Scala for Java Developers

A Practical Primer

Toby Weston

Apress®

Scala for Java Developers: A Practical Primer

Toby Weston
London, United Kingdom

ISBN-13 (pbk): 978-1-4842-3107-4   ISBN-13 (electronic): 978-1-4842-3108-1
https://doi.org/10.1007/978-1-4842-3108-1

Library of Congress Control Number: 2017963118

Cover image by Freepik (www.freepik.com)

Managing Director: Welmoed Spahr
Editorial Director: Todd Green
Acquisitions Editor: Steve Anglin
Development Editor: Matthew Moodie
Technical Reviewer: Jeff Friesen
Coordinating Editor: Mark Powers
Copy Editor: Francesca Louise White

Distributed to the book trade worldwide by Springer Science+Business Media New York, 233 Spring Street, 6th Floor, New York, NY 10013. Phone 1-800-SPRINGER, fax (201) 348-4505, e-mail orders-ny@springer-sbm.com, or visit www.springeronline.com. Apress Media, LLC is a California LLC and the sole member (owner) is Springer Science + Business Media Finance Inc (SSBM Finance Inc). SSBM Finance Inc is a **Delaware** corporation.

For information on translations, please e-mail rights@apress.com, or visit http://www.apress.com/rights-permissions.

Apress titles may be purchased in bulk for academic, corporate, or promotional use. eBook versions and licenses are also available for most titles. For more information, reference our Print and eBook Bulk Sales web page at http://www.apress.com/bulk-sales.

Any source code or other supplementary material referenced by the author in this book is available to readers on GitHub via the book's product page, located at www.apress.com/9781484231074. For more detailed information, please visit http://www.apress.com/source-code.

Printed on acid-free paper

In memory of Félix Javier García López

Table of Contents

About the Author

Toby Weston is an independent software developer based in London. He specializes in Java and Scala development, working in agile environments. He's a keen blogger and writer, having written for JAXenter and authored the books *Essential Acceptance Testing* (Leanpub) and *Learning Java Lambdas* (Packt).

About the Technical Reviewer

Jeff Friesen is a freelance teacher and software developer with an emphasis on Java. In addition to authoring *Java I/O, NIO and NIO.2* (Apress) and *Java Threads and the Concurrency Utilities* (Apress), Jeff has written numerous articles on Java and other technologies (such as Android) for JavaWorld (JavaWorld.com), informIT (informIT.com), Java.net, SitePoint (SitePoint.com), and other websites. Jeff can be contacted via his website at JavaJeff.ca. or via his LinkedIn profile (www.linkedin.com/in/javajeff).

Acknowledgments

Thanks go out to James Maggs, Alex Luker, Rhys Keepence and Xuemin Guan for their feedback on early drafts and Lee Benfield for building the excellent CFR decompiler and sharing it with the community.

Additionally, thank you to Amy Brown for providing an early copyedit of this book.

Preface

Audience

This book is for Java developers looking to transition to programming in Scala.

The Structure of the Book

The book is split into four parts: a tour of Scala, a comparison between Java and Scala, a closer look at Scala-specific features and functional programming idioms, and finally a discussion about adopting Scala into existing Java teams.

In Part I, we're going to take a high-level tour of Scala. You'll get a feel for the language's constructs and how Scala is similar in a lot of ways to Java, yet very different in others. We'll take a look at installing Scala and using the interactive interpreter and we'll go through some basic syntax examples.

Part II talks about key differences between Java and Scala. We'll look at what's missing in Scala compared to Java, vice versa, and how concepts translate from one language to another.

Then in Part III, we'll talk about some of the language features that Scala offers that aren't found in Java. This part also talks a little about functional programming idioms.

Finally, we'll talk about adopting Scala into legacy Java projects and teams. It's not always an easy transition, so we'll look at why you would want to, and some of the challenges you might face.

Compiling Code Fragments

Later in the book, I introduce the Scala REPL: an interactive tool for working with Scala and the Scala version of Java's JShell. You'll see REPL sessions prefixed with `scala>`.

When you do so, you can expect to be able to type in the code following `scala>` in the REPL verbatim, hit enter, and see the results. An example follows.

```
// an example REPL session
scala> val x = 6 * 9
x: Int = 54
```

If you don't see the `scala>` prefix, assume the fragment may depend on previous code examples. I've tried to introduce these logically, balancing the need to show complete listings with trying to avoid pages and pages of dry code listings.

If things don't make sense, always refer to the full source code. In short, you may find it useful to consult the full source while you read.

Larger Fragments in the REPL

If you'd like to transpose some of the larger code fragments into the REPL, you may notice compiler errors on hitting enter. The REPL is geared up to evaluate a line at a time. Pasting larger fragments or typing in long examples requires you to be in *paste mode*.

Typing `:paste` enters paste mode, allowing you to type multiple lines. Pressing `Ctrl + D` exits paste mode and compiles the code.

```
scala> :paste
// Entering paste mode (ctrl-D to finish)
val x = 4
val y = 34
x + y * 2
// press Ctrl + D
res1: Int = 72
```

Infrequently, you may notice an ellipsis (...) or triple question marks (???) in code fragments. When you see this, it indicates that the fragment is incomplete and will usually be followed by additional code to fill in the blanks. It probably won't compile. It's used when I've felt that additional code would be uninteresting, distracting, or when I'm building up examples.

Source Code

The source code for this book is available at GitHub: `https://github.com/tobyweston/learn-scala-java-devs`. You can clone the repository or download an archive directly from the site.

The source code is licensed under Apache 2.0 open source license.

Source Code Appendix

The book often includes partial code fragments in an attempt to avoid reams of distracting "scaffolding" code. Code may refer to previous fragments and this may not be immediately obvious. Try to read the code as if each example builds on what's gone before.

If this style isn't for you, I've also included a code listing appendix. This offers complete listings for the more complex code, in case you want to see all the code in one place. It's not there to pad out the book. Honest.

PART I

Scala Tour

Welcome to *Scala for Java Developers: A Practical Primer*. This book will help you transition from programming in Java to programming in Scala. It's designed to help Java developers get started with Scala without necessarily adopting all of the more advanced functional programming idioms.

Scala is both an object-oriented language and a functional language and, although I do talk about some of the advantages of functional programming, this book is more about being productive with imperative Scala than getting to grips with functional programming. If you're already familiar with Scala but are looking to make the leap to pure functional programming, this probably isn't the book for you. Check out the excellent *Functional Programming in Scala*[1] by Paul Chiusano and Rúnar Bjarnason instead.

The book often compares "like-for-like" between Java and Scala. So, if you're familiar with doing something a particular way in Java, I'll show how you might do the same thing in Scala. Along the way, I'll introduce the Scala language syntax.

---

[1]http://amzn.to/1Aegnwj

CHAPTER 1

The Scala Language

Scala is both a functional programming language *and* an object-oriented programming language. As a Java programmer, you'll be comfortable with the object-oriented definition: Scala has classes, objects, inheritance, composition, polymorphism—all the things you're used to in Java.

In fact, Scala goes somewhat further than Java. There are no "non"-objects. Everything is an object, so there are no primitive types like int and no static methods or fields. Functions are objects and even *values* are objects.

Scala can be accurately described as a functional programming language because it allows and promotes the use of techniques important in functional programming. It provides language level features for things like immutability and programming functions without side effects.

Traditional functional programming languages like Lisp or Haskel *only* allow you to program using these techniques. These are often referred to as *pure* functional programming languages. Scala is not *pure* in this sense; it's a hybrid. For example, you can still work with mutable data, leverage the language to work with immutable data, or do both. This is great for flexibility and easy adoption but not too great for consistency and uniformity of design.

As a Functional Programming Language

In general, functional programming languages support:

1. First-class and higher-order functions.

2. Anonymous functions (lambdas).

3. Pure functions and immutable data.

© Toby Weston 2018
T. Weston, *Scala for Java Developers*, https://doi.org/10.1007/978-1-4842-3108-1_1

It can be argued that Java supports these characteristics and certainly Java has been trying to provide better support. However, any movement in this direction has felt like an after thought and has generally resulted in verbose syntax or tension with existing idioms and language APIs.

It is unlikely that people will ever describe Java as a functional programming language despite it's advancements. Partly because it's clunky to use in this style and partly because of it's long history as an object-oriented language.

Scala on the other hand was designed as a functional programming language from day one. It has better language constructs and library support so it feels more natural when coding in a functional style. For example, it has keywords to define immutable values and the library collection classes are all immutable by default.

The Past

Scala started life in 2001 as a research project at EPFL in Switzerland. It was released publicly in 2004[2] after an internal release in 2003. The project was headed by Martin Odersky, who'd previously worked on Java generics and the Java compiler for Sun Microsystems.

It's quite rare for an academic language to cross over into industry, but Odersky and others launched Typesafe Inc. (later renamed Lightbend Inc.), a commercial enterprise built around Scala. Since then, Scala has moved firmly into the mainstream as a development language.

Scala offers a more concise syntax than Java but runs on the JVM. Running on the JVM should (in theory) mean an easy migration to production environments; if you already have the Oracle JVM installed in your production environment, it makes no difference if the bytecode was generated from the Java or Scala compiler.

It also means that Scala has Java interoperability built in, which in turn means that Scala can use any Java library. One of Java's strengths over its competitors was always the huge number of open source libraries and tools available. These are pretty much all available to Scala too. The Scala community has that same open source mentality, and so there's a growing number of excellent Scala libraries out there.

---

[2]See Odersky, "A Brief History of Scala" on Artima and wikipedia for more background.

The Future

Scala has definitely moved into the mainstream as a popular language. It has been adopted by lots of big companies including Twitter, eBay, Yahoo, HSBC, UBS, and Morgan Stanley, and it's unlikely to fall out of favour anytime soon. If you're nervous about using it in production, don't be; it's backed by an international organization and regularly scores well in popularity indexes.

The tooling is still behind Java though. Powerful IDEs like IntelliJ's IDEA and Eclipse make refactoring Java code straightforward but aren't quite there yet for Scala. The same is true of compile times: Scala is a lot slower to compile than Java. These things will improve over time and, on balance, they're not the biggest hindrances I encounter when developing.

Scala's future is tied to the future of the JVM and the JVM is still going strong. Various other functional languages are emerging however; Kotlin and Clojure in particular are interesting and may compete. If you're not interested in JVM based languages but just the benefits of functional programming, Haskel and ELM are becoming more widely adopted in industry.

CHAPTER 2

Installing Scala

Getting Started

There are a couple of ways to get started with Scala.

1. Run Scala interactively with the interpreter.

2. Run shorter programs as shell scripts.

3. Compile programs with the `scalac` compiler.

The Scala Interpreter

Before working with an IDE, it's probably worth getting familiar with the Scala interpreter, or REPL.

Download the latest Scala binaries (from `http://scala-lang.org/downloads`) and extract the archive. Assuming you have Java installed, you can start using the interpreter from a command prompt or terminal window straight away. To start up the interpreter, navigate to the exploded folder and type[3]

```
bin/scala
```

You'll be faced with the Scala prompt.

```
scala> _
```

You can type commands followed by enter, and the interpreter will evaluate the expression and print the result. It reads, evaluates, and prints in a loop so it's known as a REPL.

---

[3]If you don't want to change into the install folder to run the REPL, set the `bin` folder on your path.

© Toby Weston 2018
T. Weston, *Scala for Java Developers*, https://doi.org/10.1007/978-1-4842-3108-1_2

7

If you type 42*4 and hit enter, the REPL evaluates the input and displays the result.

```
scala> 42*4
res0: Int = 168
```

In this case, the result is assigned to a variable called res0. You can go on to use this, for example, to get half of res0.

```
scala> res0 / 2
res1: Int = 84
```

The new result is assigned to res1.

Notice the REPL also displays the type of the result: res0 and res1 are both integers (Int). Scala has inferred the types based on the values.

If you add res1 to the end of a string, no problem; the new result object is a string.

```
scala> "Hello Prisoner " + res1
res2: String = Hello Prisoner 84
```

To quit the REPL, type

```
:quit
```

The REPL is a really useful tool for experimenting with Scala without having to go to the effort of creating the usual project files. It's so useful that the community provided a Java REPL[4] as far back as 2013. Interestingly, Oracle followed suit and introduced the official Java REPL called *JShell* in Java 9 in 2017.

Scala Scripts

The creators of Scala originally tried to promote the use of Scala from Unix shell scripts. As competition to Perl, Groovy, or bash scripts on Unix environments it didn't really take off, but if you want to you can create a shell script to wrap Scala.

```
1    #!/bin/sh
2    exec scala "$0" "$@"
```

---

[4]http://www.javarepl.com/

```
3    !#
4    object HelloWorld {
5      def main(args: Array[String]) {
6        println("Hello, " + args.toList)
7      }
8    }
9    HelloWorld.main(args)
```

Don't worry about the syntax or what the script does (although I'm sure you've got a pretty good idea already). The important thing to note is that some Scala code has been embedded in a shell script and that the last line is the command to run.

You'd save it as a .sh file—for example, hello.sh—and execute it like this:

```
./hello.sh World!
```

The exec command on line 2 spawns a process to call scala with arguments; the first is the script filename itself (hello.sh) and the second is the arguments to pass to the script. The whole thing is equivalent to running Scala like this, passing in a shell script as an argument:

```
scala hello.sh World!
```

scalac

If you'd prefer, you can compile .scala files using the Scala compiler.

The scalac compiler works just like javac. It produces Java bytecode that can be executed directly on the JVM. You run the generated bytecode with the scala command. Just like Java though, it's unlikely you'll want to build your applications from the command line.

All the major IDEs support Scala projects, so you're more likely to continue using your favorite IDE. We're not going to go into the details of how to set up a Scala project in each of the major IDEs; if you're familiar with creating Java projects in your IDE, the process will be very similar.

For reference though, here are a few starting points.

- You can create bootstrap projects with Maven and the `maven-scala-plugin`.

- You can create a new Scala project directly within IntelliJ IDEA once you've installed the `scala` plugin (available in the JetBrains repository).

- Similarly, you can create a new Scala project directly within Eclipse once you have the Scala IDE plugin. Typesafe created this and it's available from the usual update sites. You can also download a bundle directly from the scala-lang or scala-ide.org sites.

- You can use SBT and create a build file to compile and run your project. SBT stands for Simple Build Tool and it's akin to Ant or Maven, but for the Scala world.

- SBT also has plugins for Eclipse and IDEA, so you can use it directly from within the IDE to create and manage the IDE project files.

CHAPTER 3

Some Basic Syntax

Defining Values and Variables

Let's look at some syntax. We'll start by creating a variable:

```
val language: String = "Scala"
```

We've defined a variable as a String and assigned to it the value of "Scala." I say "variable," but we've actually created an immutable *value* rather than a *variable*. The val keyword creates a constant, and language cannot be modified from this point on. Immutability is a key theme you'll see again and again in Scala.

If we will want to modify language later, we can use var instead of val. We can then reassign it if we need to.

```
var language: String = "Java"
language = "Scala"
```

So far, this doesn't look very different from Java. In the variable definition, the type and variable name are the opposite way around compared to Java, but that's about it. Scala uses type inference heavily, so Scala can work out that the var above is a String, even if we don't tell it.

```
val language = "Scala"
```

Notice that a semicolon isn't needed to terminate lines. The Scala compiler can generally work out when an expression is finished without needing to tell it explicitly. You only need to add semicolons when you use multiple expressions on the same line.

Operator precedence is just as you'd expect in Java. In the following example, the multiplication happens before the subtraction.

© Toby Weston 2018

T. Weston, *Scala for Java Developers*, https://doi.org/10.1007/978-1-4842-3108-1_3

```
scala> val age = 35
scala> var maxHeartRate = 210 - age * .5
res0: Double = 192.5
```

Defining Functions

Function and method definitions start with the def keyword, followed by the signature. The signature looks similar to a Java method signature but with the parameter types the other way around again, and the return type at the end rather than the start.

Let's create a function to return the minimum of two numbers.

```
def min(x: Int, y: Int): Int = {
  if (x < y)
    return x
  else
    return y
}
```

We can test it in the REPL by calling it

```
scala> min(34, 3)
res3: Int = 3
```

```
scala> min(10, 50)
res4: Int = 10
```

Note that Scala can't infer the types of function arguments.

Another trick is that you can drop the return statement. The last statement in a function will implicitly be the return value.

```
def min(x: Int, y: Int): Int = {
  if (x < y)
    x
  else
    y
}
```

Running it the REPL would show the following:

```scala
scala> min(300, 43)
res5: Int = 43
```

In this example, the `else` means the last statement is consistent with a `min` function. If I forgot the `else`, the last statement would be the same regardless and there would be a bug in our implementation:

```scala
def min(x: Int, y: Int): Int = {
  if (x < y)
    x
  y           // bug! where's the else?
}
```

It always returns y:

```scala
scala> min(10, 230)
res6: Int = 230
```

If you don't use any `return` statements, the return type can usually be inferred.

```scala
// the return type can be omitted
def min(x: Int, y: Int) = {
  if (x < y)
    x
  else
    y
}
```

Note that it's the equals sign that says this function returns something. If I write this function on one line, without the return type and just the equals sign, it starts to look like a real expression rather than a function.

```scala
def min(x: Int, y: Int) = if (x < y) x else y
```

Be wary, though; if you accidentally drop the equals sign, the function won't return anything. It'll be similar to the void in Java.

```
def min(x: Int, y: Int) {
  if (x < y) x else y
}
<console>:8: warning: a pure expression does nothing in statement position;
                    you may be omitting necessary parentheses
           if (x < y) x else y
                    ^
<console>:8: warning: a pure expression does nothing in statement position;
                    you may be omitting necessary parentheses
           if (x < y) x else y
                    ^
min: (x: Int, y: Int)Unit
```

Although this compiles okay, the compiler warns that you may have missed off the equals sign.

Operator Overloading and Infix Notation

One interesting thing to note in Scala is that you can override operators. Arithmetic operators are, in fact, just methods in Scala. As such, you can create your own. Earlier, we saw the integer age used with a multiplier.

```
val age: Int
age * .5
```

The value age is an integer and there is a method called * on the integer class. It has the following signature:

```
def *(x: Double): Double
```

Numbers are objects in Scala, as are literals. So, you can call * directly on a variable or a number.

```
age.*(.5)
5.*(10)
```

Using the *infix notation*, you're able to drop the dot notation for variables and literals and call

```
age * .5
```

...or, as another example,

```
35 toString
```

Remember, 35 is an instance of Int.

Specifically, Scala support for infix notation means that when a method takes zero or one arguments you can drop the dot and parentheses, and if there is more than one argument you can drop the dot.

For example,

```
35 + 10
"aBCDEFG" replace("a", "A")
```

It's optional though; you can use the dot notation if you prefer.

What this means is that you can define your own plus or minus method on your own classes and use it naturally with infix notation. For example, you might have a Passenger join a Train.

```
train + passenger
```

There are not many restrictions on what you can call your functions and methods; you can use any symbol that makes sense to your domain.

Collections

Scala comes with immutable collection types (like Set, List, and Map) as well as mutable versions with the same API. The creators of Scala (and the functional programming community in general) favor immutability, so when you create a collection in Scala, the immutable version is the default choice.

So, we can create a list with the following:

```
val list = List("a", "b", "c")
```

And create a map with

```
val map = Map(1 -> "a", 2 -> "b")
```

...where the arrow goes from the key to the value. These will be immutable; you won't be able to add or remove elements.

Why Favour Immutability?

Immutability is usually discussed in terms of making concurrent systems easier to reason about. This is because if shared data can be updated at the same time by multiple threads, it can be difficult to reason about and diagnose unexpected behavior such as race conditions. Removing the ability to update shared state at all can alleviate the problem; immutable objects are inherently *thread-safe*.

More generally though, immutability can lead to code that is easier to reason about even in single threaded systems. If you start out with immutable state, the design of your system is heavily influenced and you remove the chance of subtle bugs creeping in.

You can process them in a similar way to Java's forEach and lambda syntax.

```
list.foreach(value => println(value))              // scala
```

which is equivalent to the following in Java:

```
list.forEach(value -> System.out.println(value));    // java
```

Like Java's method reference syntax, you can auto-connect the lambda argument to the method call.

```
list.foreach(println)                              // scala
```

which is roughly equivalent to this Java:

```
list.forEach(System.out::println);                 // java
```

There are lots of other Scala-esque ways to process collections. We'll look at these later, but the most common way to iterate is a `for` loop written like this:

```
for (value <- list) println(value)
```

which reads, "for every value in list, print the value". You can also do it in reverse:

```
for (value <- list.reverse) println(value)
```

or you might like to break it across multiple lines:

```
for (value <- list) {
  println(value)
}
```

Tuples

A *tuple* is an ordered collection of elements. The name originates from the everyday language we use to describe multiples of things: single, pair, triple, quadruple, *n*-tuple, and so on. For example, the familiar *quadruple* is a collection of four elements. A tuple with *n* elements is an *n-tuple*. A 1-tuple is called a *single*, a 2-tuple a *pair*, a 3-tuple a *triple*, and so on. More colloquially, people refer to *n*-numbered tuples just as *tuples*. It's pronounced /tuːpəl/ and not "*tupple*".

In programming, tuples are useful to capture related values in a light-weight way without resorting to full blown objects. To capture a `String` value with a related `Int`, you'd write the following:

```
val example = ("load", 21)
```

The underlying type of the tuple in this case is a `Tuple2`, which captures the underlying types of `String` and `Int`. Where as

```
val tuple = ("save", 50, true)
```

...would result in a `Tuple3` capturing the types `String`, `Int`, and `Boolean` in that order.

Access to the values is via numbered methods prefixed with an underscore.

```scala
val event = tuple._1      // "save"
val millis = tuple._2     // 50
val success = tuple._3    // true
```

...or you can assign the values directly to variables like this:

```scala
val (event, millis, success) = tuple
```

As tuple is a type, you can refer to it as such when defining values and variables arguments to functions.

```scala
// specifying the type of the val
val save: (String, Int, Boolean) = ("save", 50, true)

// a function with a tuple as a typed argument
def audit(event: (String, Int, Boolean)) = {
  ...
}
```

Java Interoperability

I have already mentioned that you can use any Java class from Scala. For example, let's say we want to create a Java List rather than the usual Scala immutable List.

```scala
val list = new java.util.ArrayList[String]
```

All we did was fully qualify the class name (java.util.ArrayList) and use new to instantiate it. Notice the square brackets? Scala denotes generics using [ ] rather than <>. We also didn't have to use the parentheses on the constructor, as we had no arguments to pass in.

We can make method calls—for example, adding an element—just as you'd expect:

```scala
list.add("Hello")
```

...or, using infix:

```scala
list add "World!"
```

Primitive Types

In Java there are two integer types: the primitive (non-object) `int` and the `Integer` class. Scala has no concept of primitives—everything is an object—so, for example, Scala's integer type is an `Int`. Similarly, you'll be familiar with the other basic types.

Byte
Short
Int
Long
Char
String
Float
Double
Boolean

Although Scala has its own richer types, typically they just wrap the Java types. When working with these basic types, nine times out of ten you won't need to worry if you're using Scala or Java types. Things are pretty seamless. For example, Scala has a `BigDecimal` type with a + method, which means you can add two big decimals with much less code than in Java.

Compare the following Scala to Java:

```scala
// scala
val total = BigDecimal(10000) + BigDecimal(200)
```

```java
// java
BigDecimal total = new BigDecimal(10000).add(new BigDecimal(200));
```

Scala hasn't reimplemented Java's `BigDecimal`; it just delegates to it and saves you having to type all that boilerplate.

CHAPTER 4

Scala's Class Hierarchy

Scala's class hierarchy starts with the Any class in the scala package. It contains methods like ==, !=, equals, ##, hashCode, and toString.

```
abstract class Any {
  final def ==(that: Any): Boolean
  final def !=(that: Any): Boolean
  def equals(that: Any): Boolean
  def ##: Int
  def hashCode: Int
  def toString: String
  // ...
}
```

Every class in Scala inherits from the abstract class Any. It has two immediate subclasses, AnyVal and AnyRef, as shown in Figure 4-1.

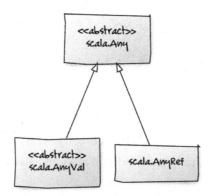

Figure 4-1. *Every class extends the Any class*

© Toby Weston 2018
T. Weston, *Scala for Java Developers*, https://doi.org/10.1007/978-1-4842-3108-1_4

AnyVal

AnyVal is the super-type to all *value types*, and AnyRef the super-type of all *reference types*.

Basic types such as Byte, Int, Char, and so on are known as value types. In Java value types correspond to the primitive types, but in Scala they are objects. Value types are all predefined and can be referred to by literals. They are usually allocated on the stack, but are allocated on the heap in Scala.

All other types in Scala are known as reference types. Reference types are objects in memory (the heap), as opposed to pointer types in C-like languages, which are addresses in memory that point to something useful and need to be dereferenced using special syntax (for example, *age = 64 in C). Reference objects are effectively dereferenced automatically.

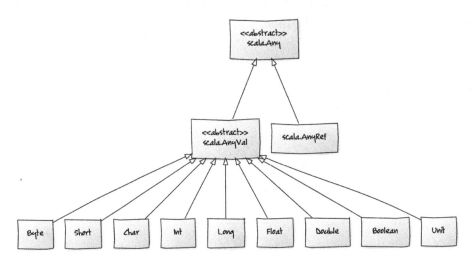

Figure 4-2. *Scala's value types*

There are nine value types in Scala, as shown in Figure 4-2.

These classes are fairly straightforward; they mostly wrap an underlying Java type and provide implementations for the == method that are consistent with Java's equals method.

This means, for example, that you can compare two number objects using == and get a sensible result, even though they may be distinct instances.

So, 42 == 42 in Scala is equivalent to creating two Integer objects in Java and comparing them with the equals method: new Integer(42).equals(new Integer(42)). You're not comparing object references, like in Java with ==, but natural equality. Remember that 42 in Scala is an instance of Int, which in turn delegates to Integer.

Unit

The Unit value type is a special type used in Scala to represent an uninteresting result. It's similar to Java's Void object or void keyword when used as a return type. It has only one value, which is written as an empty pair of brackets as follows:

```
scala> val example: Unit = ()
example: Unit = ()
```

A Java class implementing Callable with a Void object as a return would look like this:

```
// java
public class DoNothing implements Callable<Void> {
    @Override
    public Void call() throws Exception {
        return null;
    }
}
```

It is identical to this Scala class returning Unit:

```
// scala
class DoNothing extends Callable[Unit] {
  def call: Unit = ()
}
```

Remember that the last line of a Scala method is the return value, and () represents the one and only value of Unit.

AnyRef

AnyRef is an actually an alias for Java's `java.lang.Object` class. The two are interchangeable. It supplies default implementations for `toString`, `equals`, and `hashcode` for all reference types.

There used to be a subclass of `AnyRef` called `ScalaObject` that all Scala reference types extended (see Figure 4-3). However, it was only there for optimization purposes and was removed in Scala 2.11. (I mention it as a lot of documentation still refers to it.)

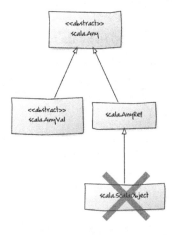

Figure 4-3. *Scala Any. The* `ScalaObject` *class no longer exists.*

The Java `String` class and other Java classes used from Scala all extend `AnyRef`. (Remember it's a synonym for `java.lang.Object`.) Any Scala-specific classes, like Scala's implementation of a list, `scala.List`, also extend `AnyRef`.

For reference types like these (shown in Figure 4-4), `==` will delegate to the `equals` method like before. For pre-existing classes like `String`, `equals` is already overridden to provide a natural notion of equality. For your own classes, you can override the `equals` just as you would in Java, but still be able to use `==` in code.

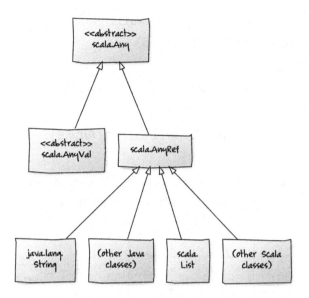

Figure 4-4. *Scala's reference types*

For example, you can compare two strings using == in Scala and it would behave just as it would in Java if you used the equals method:

```
new String("A") == new String("A")          // true in scala, false in java
new String("B").equals(new String("B"))     // true in scala and java
```

If, however, you want to revert back to Java's semantics for == and perform reference equality in Scala, you can call the eq method defined in AnyRef:

```
new String("A") eq new String("A")          // false in scala
new String("B") == new String("B")          // false in java
```

Bottom Types

A new notion to many Java developers will be the idea that a class hierarchy can have common *bottom types*. These are types that are subtypes of *all* types. Scala's types Null and Nothing are both bottom types.

All reference types in Scala are super-types of Null. Null is also an AnyRef object; it's a subclass of every reference type (see Figure 4-5).

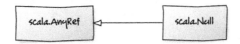

Figure 4-5. *Null extends AnyRef*

Both value and reference types are super-types of Nothing. It's at the bottom of the class hierarchy and is a subtype of all types, as shown in Figure 4-6.

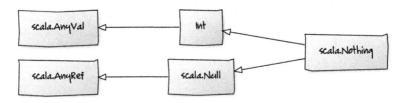

Figure 4-6. *Nothing extends Null*

Notice that Null extends all reference types and that Nothing extends all types. It's worth noting that null in Scala is an object and the single instance of the Null type. Because Null is a bottom type, null can be assigned to any reference type (AnyRef) but not subtypes of AnyVal.

This is valid:

```
val x: String = null
```

...but attempting to assign null to a Double (which extends AnyVal) causes a compiler error.

```
val x: Double = null          // compiler error
```

The entire hierarchy is shown in Figure 4-7.

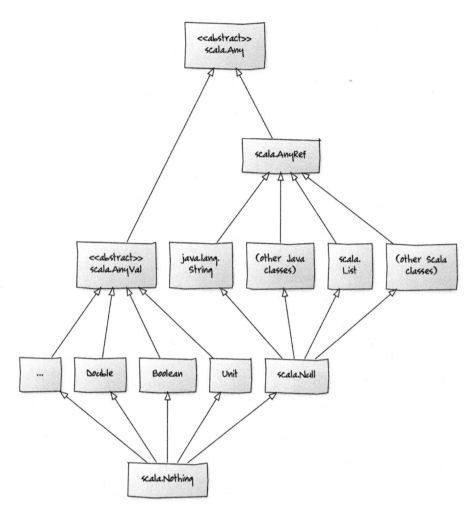

Figure 4-7. *Full hierarchy with the bottom types* Null *and* Nothing

CHAPTER 5

ScalaDoc

Scala has ported the idea of JavaDoc and creatively called it ScalaDoc. Adding ScalaDoc to your Scala source works similarly to adding JavaDoc, and is done with markup in comments (see Figure 5-1). For example, the following fragment in source code

```
/** Returns `true` if this value is equal to x, `false` otherwise. **/
def ==(x: Byte): Boolean
```

...can be turned into the following fragment in HTML:

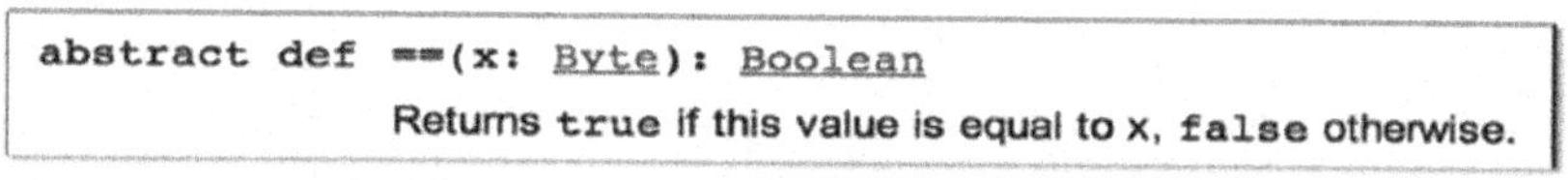

```
abstract def ==(x: Byte): Boolean
                Returns true if this value is equal to x, false otherwise.
```

Figure 5-1. *Embedded ScalaDoc markup gets rendered in HTML*

To see the documentation for the Scala Library API, head over to the Scala website.[5] You'll notice it is broadly similar to JavaDoc. You can see the classes along the left; they're not grouped by package like in JavaDoc but they're clickable to get more information.

---

[5]http://docs.scala-lang.org/api/all.html

© Toby Weston 2018

T. Weston, *Scala for Java Developers*, https://doi.org/10.1007/978-1-4842-3108-1_5

29

A neat feature of ScalaDoc is that you can also filter the content. For example, you can show only methods inherited from Any.

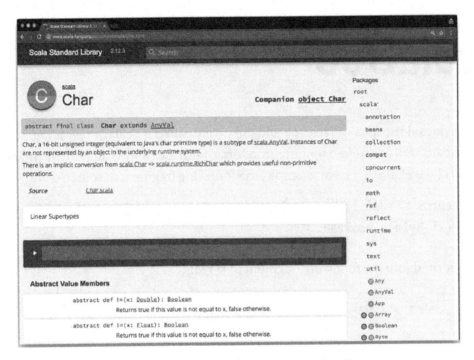

Figure 5-2. *The basic ScalaDoc for* Char

If you're interested in the hierarchy of a class, you can look at its super-types and subtypes. You may even see a navigable diagram of the type hierarchy, although not every class has this. The type hierarchy diagram for Source in Figure 5-3 shows it is a subtype of Iterable and Closable, and you can navigate up through the hierarchy by clicking on the diagram.

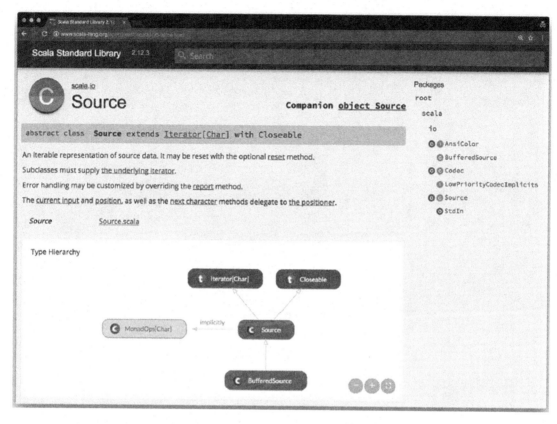

Figure 5-3. *ScalaDoc showing the type hierarchy diagram*

CHAPTER 6

Language Features

On our tour we've seen some example syntax, walked through the class hierarchy, and briefly looked at ScalaDoc, but Scala offers heaps of other interesting language features.

In this chapter, we won't really talk about syntax but we'll discuss some of the things that make Scala an interesting and powerful language when working with source code, working with methods, and using its functional programming features.

Working with Source Code

Source Files. What you put in source files is much more flexible in Scala than in Java. While in Java a file must be named the same as the public class it contains, there's no such restriction for `.scala` files. A file called `Customer.scala` might contain a class called `Customer`, but it doesn't have to. Similarly, it might contain four classes, none of which is called `Customer`.

Packages. Although essentially the same thing as in Java, classes in packages don't have to live in folders of the same name like they do in Java. There are some differences in scoping—for example, there's no `protected` keyword in Scala but you can use special syntax (`variable[package]`) to achieve the same thing.

Package objects. Scala also has the idea of *package objects*. These are objects that you can put useful chunks of code in, for reuse within the package scope. They're available to other classes in the package, and if someone imports that package, everything within the package object is available to them too. Libraries often use these to allow you to import all their classes in one go.

Import alias. Imports are about the same as in Java, but once you've imported a class in Scala, you can rename it within your class. In other words, you can create an alias for a class within your class. This can be useful when you've got a name clash—for example, between libraries.

© Toby Weston 2018
T. Weston, *Scala for Java Developers*, https://doi.org/10.1007/978-1-4842-3108-1_6

Type aliases. Scala also supports type aliases. You can give an alias to a complex type definition to help clarify the intent. It's similar to a structureless `typedef` or `#define` macro in C, or what's called *type synonyms* in Haskell.

Traits. Although Scala has classes and objects, there is no "interface" keyword. Instead, there is the idea of a `trait` that is similar to an interface but can have methods. It's somewhere between Java 8's default methods and Ruby's mixins.

Working with Methods

Generics. There's better support for generic type covariance and contravariance in Scala than Java. This means that you can be more general and more flexible in your method signatures when generic types are used as arguments. Don't worry about the specifics just yet, there's a whole section on variance later.

> ### Variance In-Brief
>
> Covariance of generic *types* means that, if the generic parameter of a type (the bit in brackets like <T>) is a subtype of something, then the generic type itself is also a subtype of another generic type when that type's parameter is the super-type. For example, a List<Cat> would also be (subtype of) a List<Animal> assuming Cat extends Animal. Contravariance also preserves the relationship but this time in reverse. Java doesn't support type variance like this but does support covariant return types. Method arguments and variables can also be covariant or contravariant in both Scala and Java.

Variable arguments. When working with methods, Scala supports variable arguments or `varargs` just like Java.

```
public void add(String... names)    // java
def add(names: String*)             // scala
```

Named method arguments. Something Java doesn't offer is named method arguments. In Scala, you can call a method with its arguments out of order, as long as you name them. So, given the function def swap(first: Int, second: Int), you can call it explicitly, naming its arguments. Because they're named, the compiler can work out which is which regardless of their position. So, the following is fine:

```
swap(first = 3, second = 1)
swap(second = 1, first = 3)
```

Default values. You can add a default value by using = after the parameter declaration. For example, def swap(first: Int, second: Int = 1). The second value will default to 1 if you leave it off when you call the function. You can still supply a value to override the default, and still use named parameters.

```
swap(3)
swap(3, 2)
swap(first = 3)
swap(first = 3, second = 1)
```

Function literals. A function literal is just an expression that creates an unnamed function. You can store these as variables, pass them around, or pass them into methods. Creating them on the fly means you can create succinct bits of functionality without the boilerplate. A functional literal is a way to refer to a lambda.

Lambdas. Scala supports lambdas or anonymous functions. You can pass function literals as arguments to methods and use a function signature as an argument in a method signature. So, the test method that follows takes a function with no arguments, which returns a Boolean.

```
def test(f: () => Boolean) = ...
```

When you call it, you can pass in a function literal as a parameter.

```
test(() => if (!tuesday) true else false)
```

As another example, you can create a function signature to represent a function from a String value to a Boolean like this:

```
def test(f: String => Boolean): Boolean = ...
```

...and call it with a function literal like this:

```
test(value => if (value == "tuesday") true else false)
```

Functional Programming

There are some other Scala features aimed more at functional programming.

Pattern matching. This is a hugely powerful feature, which at first blush looks similar to switches but can be used for much more.

For comprehensions. These are subtly different from regular for loops, and are useful when working with functional constructs. When you first encounter them, they'll look like an alternative syntax to Java's `for` loop.

Currying. Although you can write your own currying functions in any language, Scala supports currying as a language feature. If you're unsure what currying is, you don't need to worry about it right now. See the currying section for more details.

Functional literals. The language supports literals to represent some useful types like tuples. Popular Java functional libraries like totally-lazy[6] or functional-java[7] have these kinds of things; Scala just makes them easier to work with.

Recursion. Most languages support recursion, but Scala has compiler support for tail call optimization, which means it can support recursive calls that would result in a stack overflow in languages like Java. The compiler can even perform some checks for you if you use the `@tailrec` annotation.

---

[6]`http://totallylazy.com/`
[7]`http://www.functionaljava.org/`

CHAPTER 7

Summary

In this high-level tour, we talked about how Scala is both an OO language and a functional language. I mentioned that Scala in fact only has objects; there are no primitives, everything is an object.

We talked about Scala's background, how it grew from an academic language to a commercially backed mainstream language, and how it runs on the JVM. This, in theory, lowers the barrier of adoption by making it easy to deploy to existing servers.

Running on the JVM also means there are plenty of libraries available to Scala, as Java interoperability is baked in. Despite some of the tools being behind and compilation time still being slow, Scala has been widely adopted and we see numerous big companies using it today.

We had a look at installing and running Scala. You saw the three ways Scala programs are typically run, and along the way were introduced to the Scala REPL.

We then moved on to a syntax tour and looked at some interesting language features.

In the syntax tour, we saw how to define variables and values, functions and methods, and saw how Scala reduces the boilerplate noise by inferring types and recognizing terminating conditions like `return` and semicolons automatically.

We saw how infix notation means you can avoid the classical dot notation and, importantly, we saw that method names can contain symbols. That's how we're able to use mathematical symbols naturally in code; they're actually methods, so we can override them and, using the infix notation, use them without the noisy dots and brackets.

We also worked with some collection types and saw a couple of basic ways to enumerate them: the `foreach` and `for` loop syntax. We saw how easy it is to work with Java objects; value types like `Int` and `Boolean` are basically the same in Scala and Java. We had a good look at how Scala represents types in its class hierarchy, and learnt how to look things up in the ScalaDoc.

© Toby Weston 2018
T. Weston, *Scala for Java Developers*, https://doi.org/10.1007/978-1-4842-3108-1_7

In terms of language features, we looked at some interesting aspects of the language when working with source files and packages, methods and method arguments, as well as some features geared up for functional programming.

PART II

Key Syntactical Differences

This part of the book is about the key differences between Java and Scala language syntax. Given some typical Java code, we'll look at equivalent Scala syntax. In Part III, we'll look more at Scala features for which there is no direct equivalent in Java.

We're going to look at the following:

- Lots of things around classes and objects, creating classes, fields, and methods. We'll do some round-tripping from Scala-generated bytecode back to Java, so that you can get a feel for how Scala relates to Java.

- Inheritance, interfaces, abstract classes, and mixins.

- Common control structures like for loops.

- Generics.

Flexibility

Scala is very flexible. There are generally several ways to achieve the same thing. I don't mean the difference between using a while loop or for loop; I mean that the language has different syntax options for expressing the same thing. This flexibility gives a lot of freedom but can be confusing when you're reading code from different authors.

An example is the infix notation we saw earlier. You can often drop the dots and brackets when calling methods. Scala is opinion-less; it's up to you if you want to use the dots or not.

Java, on the other hand, is very restrictive; there are generally very few ways to express the same things. It's often easier to recognize things at a glance. You might have to work a little harder to recognize some of the more exotic syntax options in Scala.

This is true when it comes to the structure of your code too; you can create functions within functions, import statements in the middle of a class, or have a class live in a file with an unrelated name. It can all be a little disorienting when you're used to the rigidity of Java.

Immutable and Declarative

Because Scala favors immutability, you might also notice a different approach to solving problems. For example, you might notice a lack of looping over mutable variables. Scala programs usually favor more functional idioms to achieve the same thing.

This more *declarative* way of doing things says "tell me what to do, not how to do it." You may be more used to the Java/imperative way of doing things that says "tell me exactly how to do it". Ultimately, when you give up the micro-management style of imperative programming, you allow the language more freedom in how it goes about its business.

For example, a traditional imperative for loop in Java looks like this:

```java
// java
for (int count = 0; count < 100; count++) {
    System.out.println(count);
}
```

It's a typical imperative loop. We're telling it explicitly to enumerate serially from zero to one hundred. If, on the other hand, we use a more declarative mechanism, like this:

```scala
// scala
(0 to 100).foreach(println(_))
```

...the enumeration is done within the foreach method, not by a language construct. We're saying, "for a range of numbers, perform some function on each." Although only subtly different, we're not saying *how* to enumerate the sequence. It means Scala is free to implement the enumeration however it likes. It may choose to do it in parallel, for example.

Interestingly, Oracle has adopted these ideas and since Java 8 offers similar for loop enumeration. The preceding code can be written in Java like this:

```
// java
IntStream.range(0, 100).forEach(System.out::println)
```

CHAPTER 8

Classes and Fields

In this chapter, we'll have a look at the following:

1.   Creating classes.

2.   How Scala makes things easier when defining fields.

3.   What happens behind the scenes when Scala creates methods for you.

Creating Classes

Creating a class in Java means writing something like this:

```java
// java
public class Customer {
}
```

It makes sense for us to have a name and address for a customer. So, adding these as fields and initializing via the constructor would give us something like this:

```java
// java
public class Customer {
    private final String name;
    private final String address;

    public Customer(String name, String address) {
        this.name = name;
        this.address = address;
    }
}
```

© Toby Weston 2018
T. Weston, *Scala for Java Developers*, https://doi.org/10.1007/978-1-4842-3108-1_8

We can instantiate an instance with the new keyword and create a new customer called Eric like this:

```
Customer eric = new Customer("Eric", "29 Acacia Road"); // java
```

In Scala, the syntax is much briefer; we can combine the class and constructor on a single line.

```
class Customer(val name: String, val address: String)   // scala
```

We new it up in the same way, like this:

```
val eric = new Customer("Eric", "29 Acacia Road")        // scala
```

Rather than define the fields as members within the class, the Scala version declares the variables as part of the class definition in what's known as the *primary constructor*. In one line, we've declared the class Customer and, in effect, declared a constructor with two arguments.

Derived Setters and Getters

The val keyword on the class definition tells the compiler to treat the arguments as fields. It will create the fields and accessor methods for them.

We can prove this by taking the generated class file and decompiling it into Java. Round-tripping like this is a great way to explore what Scala actually produces behind the scenes. I've used the excellent CFR decompiler[8] by Lee Benfield here, but you could also use the javap program that ships with Java to get the basic information.

To run the decompiler on the Scala generated class file for Customer, you do something like the following:

```
java -jar cfr_0_122.jar target/scala-2.12/classes/s4j/scala/chapter09/
Customer.class
```

---

[8]http://www.benf.org/other/cfr/

It produces the following:

```
1    // decompiled from scala to java
2    public class Customer {
3        private final String name;
4        private final String address;
5
6        public String name() {
7            return this.name;
8        }
9
10       public String address() {
11           return this.address;
12       }
13
14       public Customer(String name, String address) {
15           this.name = name;
16           this.address = address;
17       }
18   }
```

What's important to notice is that Scala has generated accessor methods at lines 6 and 10, and a constructor at line 14. The accessors aren't using the Java getter convention, but we've got the equivalent of getName and getAddress.

You might also want to define fields but not have them set via the constructor. For example, in Java, we might want to add an id to the customer to be set later with a setter method. This is a common pattern for tools like Hibernate when populating an object from the database.

```
// java
public class Customer {
    private final String name;
    private final String address;

    private String id;

    public Customer(String name, String address) {
        this.name = name;
```

```
        this.address = address;
    }

    public void setId(String id) {
        this.id = id;
    }
}
```

Is Scala, you do pretty much the same thing.

```scala
// scala
class Customer(val name: String, val address: String) {
  var id = ""
}
```

You define a field, in this case a var, and magically Scala will create a setter method for you. The setter method it creates is called id_= rather than the usual setId. If we round-trip this through the decompiler, we see the following:

```java
1   // decompiled from scala to java
2   public class Customer {
3       private final String name;
4       private final String address;
5       private String id;
6
7       public String name() {
8           return this.name;
9       }
10      public String address() {
11          return this.address;
12      }
13      public String id() {                      // notice it's public
14          return this.id;
15      }
16      public void id_$eq(String x$1) {          // notice it's public
17          this.id = x$1;
18      }
19      public Customer(String name, String address) {
```

```
20          this.name = name;
21          this.address = address;
22          this.id = null;
23      }
24  }
```

Notice it has created a method called id_$eq on line 16 rather than id_=; that's because the equals symbol isn't allowed in a method name on the JVM, so Scala has escaped it and will translate it as required. You can call the setter method directly like this:

```
new Customer("Bob", "10 Downing Street").id_=("000001")
```

Scala offers a shorthand; however, you can just use regular assignment and Scala will call the auto-generated id_$eq setter method under the covers:

```
new Customer("Bob", "10 Downing Street").id = "000001"
```

If there are no access modifiers in front of a field, the field becomes public. So, as well as being able to call the auto-generated setter, clients could also work directly on the field, potentially breaking encapsulation. We'd like to be able to make the field private and allow updates only from within the Customer class.

To do this, just use the private keyword with the field.

```
class Customer(val name: String, val address: String) {
  private var id = ""
}
```

The decompiler shows that the setter and getter methods are now private.

```
1   // decompiled from scala to java
2   public class Customer {
3       private final String name;
4       private final String address;
5       private String id;
6
7       public String name() {
8           return this.name;
9       }
10
```

47

```
11      public String address() {
12          return this.address;
13      }
14
15      private String id() {                    // now it's private
16          return this.id;
17      }
18
19      private void id_$eq(String x$1) {        // now it's private
20          this.id = x$1;
21      }
22
23      public Customer(String name, String address) {
24          this.name = name;
25          this.address = address;
26          this.id = "";
27      }
28  }
```

Redefining Setters and Getters

The advantage of using setters to set values is that we can use the method to preserve invariants or perform special processing. In Java, it's straightforward: you create the setter method in the first place. It's more laborious for Scala, as the compiler generates the methods and you are forced to redefine them.

For example, once the id has been set, we might want to prevent it from being updated. In Java, we could do something like this:

```
// java
public void setId(String id) {
    if (id.isEmpty())
        this.id = id;
}
```

Scala, on the other hand, creates the setter method automatically, so how do we redefine it? If we try to just replace the setter directly in the Scala code, we'd get a compiler error like this:

```scala
// scala doesn't compile
class Customer(val name: String, val address: String) {
  private var id = ""

  def id_=(value: String) {
    if (id.isEmpty)
      this.id = value
  }
}
```

Scala can't know to replace the method so it creates a *second method* of the same name, and the compiler fails when it sees the duplicate.

```
ambiguous reference to overloaded definition,
both method id_= in class Customer of type (value: String)Unit
and method id_= in class Customer of type (x$1: String)Unit
match argument types (String)
  this.id = value

method id_= is defined twice
  conflicting symbols both originated in file 'Customer.scala'
  def id_=(value: String) {
      ^         ^
```

To redefine the method, we have to jump through some hoops. Firstly, we have to rename the field (say to _id), making it private so as to make the getter and setter private. Then we create a new getter method called id and setter method called id_= that are public and are used to access the renamed private field.

```scala
class Customer(val name: String, val address: String) {
  private var _id: String = ""

  def id = _id

  def id_=(value: String) {
    if (_id.isEmpty)
```

```
        _id = value
    }
}
```

We've hidden the real field _id behind the private modifier and exposed a method called id_= to act as a setter. As there is no field called id any more, Scala won't try to generate the duplicate method, and things compile.

```
// REPL session
scala> val bob = new Customer("Bob", "32 Bread Street")
bob: Customer = Customer@e955027

scala> bob.id = "001"
bob.id: String = 001

scala> println(bob.id)
001
scala> bob.id = "002"
bob.id: String = 001
scala> println(bob.id)
001
```

Looking at the decompiled version, you can see how to redefine the method. We've hidden the real field and exposed public methods to synthesize access to it under the guise of the field name.

```
1   // decompiled from scala to java
2   public class Customer {
3       private final String name;
4       private final String address;
5       private String _id;
6
7       public String name() {
8           return this.name;
9       }
10
```

```
11        public String address() {
12            return this.address;
13        }
14
15        private String _id() {                     // private
16            return this._id;
17        }
18
19        private void _id_$eq(String x$1) {         // private
20            this._id = x$1;
21        }
22
23        public String id() {                       // public
24            return this._id();
25        }
26
27        public void id_$eq(String value) {         // public
28            if (!this._id().isEmpty()) return;
29            this._id_$eq(value);
30        }
31
32        public Customer(String name, String address) {
33            this.name = name;
34            this.address = address;
35            this._id = "";
36        }
37    }
```

Why The Getter?

You might be wondering why we created the getter method def id(). Scala won't allow us to use the shorthand assignment syntax to set a value unless the class has both the setter (id_=) and getter methods defined.

Redefining setters and getters is fairly common in Java but, in practice, is less so in Scala. Although this section may seem a bit academic, if you do try to redefine these methods in Scala and encounter unexpected compiler errors, you'll at least understand why.

Summary

Creating classes is straightforward with Scala. You can add fields to the class simply by adding parameters to the class definition, and the equivalent Java constructor, getters, and setters are generated for you by the compiler.

All fields in the class file are generated as private but have associated accessor methods generated. These generated methods are affected by the presence of val or var in the class definition.

- If val is used, a public getter is created but no setter is created. The value can only be set by the constructor.

- If var is used, a public getter and setter are created. The value can be set via the setter or the constructor.

- If neither val or var is used, no methods are generated and the value can only be used within the scope of the primary constructor; it's not really a field in this case.

- Prefixing the class definition with private won't change these rules, but it will make any generated methods private.

This is summarized in Table 8-1.

Table 8-1. *Generated methods*

class Foo(? x)	val x	var x	x	private val x	private var x
Getter created (x())	Y (public)	Y (public)	N	Y (private)	Y (private)
Setter created (x_=(y))	N	Y (public)	N	N	Y (private)
Generated constructor includes x	Y	Y	N	Y	Y

If you need to override the generated methods, you have to rename the field and mark it as private. You then recreate the getter and setter methods with the original name. In practice, it's not something you'll have to do very often.

CHAPTER 9

Classes and Objects

In this chapter we'll look at the following:

- How you can define fields within the class body rather than on the class definition line and how this affects the generated methods.

- How you create additional constructors.

- Scala's singleton objects defined with the object keyword.

- *Companion objects*, a special type of singleton object.

Classes Without Constructor Arguments

Let's begin by looking at how we create fields within classes without defining them on the class definition line. If you were to create a class in Scala with no fields defined on the class definition, like this:

```scala
// scala
class Counter
```

...the Scala compiler would still generate a primary constructor with no arguments, a lot like Java's default constructor. So, the Java equivalent would look like this:

```java
// java
public class Counter {
    public Counter() {
    }
}
```

© Toby Weston 2018
T. Weston, *Scala for Java Developers*, https://doi.org/10.1007/978-1-4842-3108-1_9

In Java you might initialize a variable and create some methods.

```java
// java
public class Counter {

    private int count = 0;

    public Counter() {
    }

    public void increment() {
        count++;
    }

    public int getCount() {
        return count;
    }
}
```

You can do the same in Scala.

```scala
// scala
class Counter {
  private var count = 0

  def increment() {
    count += 1
  }

  def getCount = count
}
```

Within the primary constructor (that is, not in the class definition but immediately afterwards in the class body), the val and var keywords may generate getters and setters. Their presence affects the bytecode as shown in Table 9-1.

Table 9-1. *How the presence of getters and setters affects the bytecode*

Declared in primary constructor	val x	var x	x	private val x	private var x
Getter (x())	Y (public)	Y (public)	N/A	Y (private)	Y (private)
Setter (x_=(y))	N	Y (public)	N/A	N	Y (private)

As you can see, this is consistent with Table 8-1. Getters are generated by default for val and var types and will all be public. Adding private to the field declaration will make the generated fields private and setters are only generated for vars (which are, again, public by default).

Additional Constructors

Let's create an alternative Java version of our Customer class, this time with additional constructors.

```java
// java
public class Customer {

    private final String fullname;

    public Customer(String forename, String initial, String surname) {
        this.fullname =
            String.format("%s %s. %s", forename, initial, surname);
    }

    public Customer(String forename, String surname) {
        this(forename, "", surname);
    }
}
```

We've defaulted the customer's initial and allowed clients to choose if they want to supply it.

We should probably tidy up the main constructor to reflect the fact that the variable could come through as an empty string. We'll add an if-condition and format the string depending on the result.

```java
// java
public class Customer {
    private final String fullname;

    public Customer(String forename, String initial, String surname) {
        if (initial != null && !initial.isEmpty())
            this.fullname =
                String.format("%s %s. %s", forename, initial, surname);
        else
            this.fullname = String.format("%s %s", forename, surname);
    }

    public Customer(String forename, String surname) {
        this(forename, "", surname);
    }

    public static void main(String... args) {
        System.out.println(new Customer("Bob", "J", "Smith").fullname);
        System.out.println(new Customer("Bob", "Smith").fullname);
    }
}
```

Creating additional or *auxiliary constructors* in Scala is just a matter of creating methods called this. The one constraint is that each auxiliary constructor must call another constructor using this on its first line. That way, constructors will always be chained, all the way to the top.

Scala has the notion of a *primary constructor*; it's the code in the class body. Any parameters passed in from the class definition are available to it. If you don't write any auxiliary constructors, the class will still have a constructor; it's the implicit primary constructor.

```scala
// scala
class Customer(forename: String, initial: String, surname: String) {
    // primary constructor
}
```

So, if we create a field within the primary constructor and assign it some value,

```scala
// scala
class Customer(forename: String, initial: String, surname: String) {
  val fullname = String.format("%s %s. %s", forename, initial, surname)
}
```

...it would be equivalent to the following Java:

```java
// java
public class Customer {
    private final String fullname;

    public Customer(String forename, String initial, String surname) {
        this.fullname =
            String.format("%s %s. %s", forename, initial, surname);
    }
}
```

If we can add another auxiliary constructor to the Scala version, we can refer to this to chain the call to the primary constructor.

```scala
// scala
class Customer(forename: String, initial: String, surname: String) {
  val fullname = String.format("%s %s. %s", forename, initial, surname)

  def this(forename: String, surname: String) {
    this(forename, "", surname)
  }
}
```

Using Default Values

Scala has language support for default values on method signatures, so we could have written this using just parameters on the class definition, and avoided the extra constructor. We'd just default the value for initial to be an empty string. To make the implementation handle empty strings better, we can put some logic in the primary constructor like in the Java version before.

```scala
class Customer(forename: String, initial: String = "", surname: String) {
  val fullname = if (initial != null && !initial.isEmpty)
    forename + " " + initial + "." + surname
  else
    forename + " " + surname
}
```

When calling it, we would need to name default values when we don't supply all the arguments in the order they're declared. For example:

```scala
new Customer("Bob", "J", "Smith")
```

"Bob", "J", "Smith" is ok, but if we skip the initial variable, we'd need to name the surname variable like this:

```scala
new Customer("Bob", surname = "Smith")
```

Singleton Objects

In Java you can enforce a single instance of a class using the singleton pattern. Scala has adopted this idea as a feature of the language itself: as well as classes, you can define (singleton) *objects*.

The downside is that when we talk about "objects" in Scala, we're overloading the term. We might mean an instance of a class (for example, a new ShoppingCart(), of which there could be many) or we might mean the one and only instance of a class; that is, a singleton object.

A typical use-case for a singleton in Java is if we need to use a single logger instance across an entire application.

```java
// java
Logger.getLogger().log(INFO, "Everything is fine.");
```

We might implement the singleton like this:

```java
// java
public final class Logger {

    private static final Logger INSTANCE = new Logger();

    private Logger() { }
```

```java
public static Logger getLogger() {
    return INSTANCE;
}

public void log(Level level, String string) {
    System.out.printf("%s %s%n", level, string);
}
}
```

We create a Logger class, and a single static instance of it. We prevent anyone else creating one by using a private constructor. We then create an accessor to the static instance, and finally give it a rudimentary log method. We'd call it like this:

```java
// java
Logger.getLogger().log(INFO, "Singleton loggers say YEAH!");
```

A more concise way to achieve the same thing in Java would be to use an enum.

```java
// java
public enum LoggerEnum {

    LOGGER;

    public void log(Level level, String string) {
        System.out.printf("%s %s%n", level, string);
    }
}
```

We don't need to use an accessor method; Java ensures a single instance is used and we'd call it like this:

```java
// java
LOGGER.log(INFO, "An alternative example using an enum");
```

Either way, they prevent clients newing up an instance of the class and provide a single, global instance for use.

The Scala equivalent would look like this:

```scala
// scala
object Logger {
  def log(level: Level, string: String) {
```

```
    printf("%s %s%n", level, string)
  }
}
```

The thing to notice here is that the singleton instance is denoted by the object keyword rather than class. So, we're saying "define a single object called Logger" rather than "define a class".

Under the covers, Scala is creating basically the same Java code as our singleton pattern example. You can see this when we decompile it.

```
1   // decompiled from scala to java
2   public final class Logger$ {
3       public static final Logger$ MODULE$;
4
5       public static {
6           new scala.demo.singleton.Logger$();
7       }
8
9       public void log(Level level, String string) {
10          Predef..MODULE$.printf("%s %s%n", (Seq)Predef..MODULE$
11          .genericWrapArray((Object)new Object[]{level, string}));
12      }
13
14      private Logger$() {
15          Logger$.MODULE$ = this;
16      }
17  }
```

There are some oddities in the log method, but that's the decompiler struggling to decompile the bytecode, and generally how Scala goes about things. In essence though, it's equivalent; there's a private constructor like the Java version, and a single static instance of the object. The class itself is even final.

There's no need to new up a new Logger; Logger is already an object, so we can refer to it directly. In fact, you couldn't new one up if you wanted to, because the generated constructor is private.

A method on a Scala *object* is equivalent to static methods in Java. An example is the static `main` method on a Java class that can be executed by the runtime. You create a `main` method in a Scala singleton object, not a class to replicate the behavior.

Companion Objects

You can combine objects and classes in Scala. When you create a class and an object with the same name in the same source file, the *object* is known as a *companion object*.

Scala doesn't have a `static` keyword but members of singleton objects are effectively static. Remember that a Scala singleton object is just that, a singleton. Any members it contains will therefore be reused by all clients using the object; they're globally available just like statics.

You use companion objects where you would mix statics and non-statics in Java.

The Java version of `Customer` has fields for the customer's name and address, and an ID to identify the customer uniquely.

```java
// java
public class Customer {

    private final String name;
    private final String address;

    private Integer id;

    public Customer(String name, String address) {
        this.name = name;
        this.address = address;
    }
}
```

Now we may want to create a helper method to create the next ID in a sequence. To do that globally, we create a static field to capture a value for the ID and a method to return and increment it. We can then just call the method on construction of a new instance, assigning its ID to the freshly incremented global ID.

```java
// java
public class Customer {

    private static Integer lastId;

    private final String name;
    private final String address;

    private Integer id;

    public Customer(String name, String address) {
        this.name = name;
        this.address = address;
        this.id = Customer.nextId();
    }

    private static Integer nextId() {
        return lastId++;
    }

}
```

It's static because we want to share its implementation among all instances to create globally unique IDs for each.

In Scala, we'd separate the static from non-static members and put the statics in the singleton object and the rest in the class. The singleton object is the *companion object* to Customer.

We create our class with the two required fields and in the singleton object, create the nextId method. Next, we create a private var to capture the current value, assigning it the value of zero so Scala can infer the type as an Integer. Adding a val here means no setter will be generated, and adding the private modifier means the generated getter will be private. We finish off by implementing the increment in the nextId method and calling it from the primary constructor.

```scala
// scala
class Customer(val name: String, val address: String) {
  private val id = Customer.nextId()
}
```

```
object Customer {
  private var lastId = 0

  private def nextId(): Integer = {
    lastId += 1
    lastId
  }
}
```

The singleton object is a *companion object* because it has the same name and lives in the same source file as its class. This means the two have a special relationship and can access each other's private members. That's how the Customer object can define the nextId method as private but the Customer *class* can still access it.

If you were to name the object differently, you wouldn't have this special relationship and wouldn't be able to call the method. For example, the class CustomerX object that follows is not a companion object to Customer and so can't see the private nextId method.

```
// scala
class Customer(val name: String, val address: String) {
  private val id = CustomerX.nextId()        // compiler failure
}

object CustomerX {
  private var lastId = 0

  private def nextId(): Integer = {
    lastId += 1
    lastId
  }
}
```

Other Uses for Companion Objects

When methods don't depend on any of the fields in a class, you can more accurately think of them as functions. Functions generally belong in a singleton object rather than a class, so one example of when to use companion objects is when you want to distinguish between functions and methods, but keep related functions close to the class they relate to.

Another reason to use a companion object is for factory-style methods—methods that create instances of the class companion. For example, you might want to create a factory method that creates an instance of your class but with less noise. If we want to create a factory for Customer, we can do so like this:

```scala
// scala
class Customer(val name: String, val address: String) {
  val id = Customer.nextId()
}

object Customer {
  def apply(name: String, address: String) = new Customer(name, address)
  def nextId() = 1
}
```

The apply method affords a shorthand notation for a class or object. It's kind of like the default method for a class, so if you don't call a method directly on an instance, but instead match the arguments of an apply method, it'll call it for you. For example, you can call:

```scala
Customer.apply("Bob Fossil", "1 London Road")
```

...or you can drop the apply and Scala will look for an apply method that matches your argument. The two are identical.

```scala
Customer("Bob Fossil", "1 London Road")
```

You can still construct a class using the primary constructor and new, but implementing the companion class apply method as a factory means you can be more concise if you have to create a lot of objects.

You can even force clients to use your factory method rather than the constructor by making the primary constructor private.

```scala
class Customer private (val name: String, val address: String) {
  val id = Customer.nextId()
}
```

The Java analog would have a static factory method—for example, createCustomer—and a private constructor ensuring everyone is forced to use the factory method.

```java
// java
public class Customer {

    private static Integer lastId;

    private final String name;
    private final String address;

    private Integer id;

    public static Customer createCustomer(String name, String address) {
        return new Customer(name, address);
    }

    private Customer(String name, String address) {
        this.name = name;
        this.address = addres s;
        this.id = Customer.nextId();
    }

    private static Integer nextId() {
        return lastId++;
    }
}
```

CHAPTER 10

Classes and Functions

In this chapter we'll look at the following:

- Anonymous functions or *lambdas*.

- How anonymous classes differ from anonymous functions.

- First-class and higher-order functions.

- The differences between a function and a method.

- The differences between lambdas and closures.

Anonymous Functions

A function in the general sense is a code fragment designed to perform a specific task or calculation. You can create a function as a Java method or a Scala `def`. Both by their nature are *named*. Anonymous functions, on the other hand, do not have a name.

An anonymous function is also called a *lambda* and when used can be referred to as a *function literal*.

Java lambda syntax starts by listing the arguments to the function then the arrow token followed by the implementation body. The following example is a lambda taking two string arguments and comparing their values for a sorting algorithm.

```java
// java
(String a, String b) -> {
    int comparison = a.compareTo(b);
    return comparison;
};
```

© Toby Weston 2018
T. Weston, *Scala for Java Developers*, https://doi.org/10.1007/978-1-4842-3108-1_10

If the compiler can infer the types of the argument, you can drop the types and, if the body is a single line expression, you can drop the `return`.

```
(a, b) -> a.compareTo(b);        // abbreviated form
```

For single argument lambdas, you can even drop the parameter parenthesis but if there are no arguments, you need empty parenthesis.

```
value -> value * 2;              // single argument
() -> 2 + 2;                     // no arguments
```

In Scala, a lambda looks very similar. As the last statement in an expression is assumed to be the return value, the `return` keyword is not required.

```
// scala
(a: String, b: String) => {
  val comparison = a.compareTo(b)
  comparison
}
```

If Scala can infer the arguments, the types can be dropped as in Java and single line expressions don't require braces.

```
// scala
(a, b) => a.compareTo(b)         // abbreviated form
```

Anonymous classes can be used to provide functionality in a similar way to anonymous functions but they can not accurately be called lambdas.

Anonymous Classes

An anonymous class isn't the same thing as an anonymous function. An anonymous class still needs to be instantiated to an object via the new keyword. It may not have a name but it's only useful when it's an *instance object*.

An anonymous function, on the other hand, has no instance associated with it. Functions are disassociated with the data they act on.

A typical anonymous class in Java might look like this:

```java
// java
List<String> list = Arrays.asList("A", "C", "B", "D");
list.sort(new Comparator<String>() {
    @Override
    public int compare(String a, String b) {
        return a.compareTo(b);
    }
});
```

You can still create anonymous classes in Scala but you don't often need to. In Scala it's more common to create an anonymous function or lambda. Indeed, since the introduction of lambdas in Java 8, the same is also true of Java.

```scala
// scala
val list = List("A", "C", "B", "D")
list.sorted(new Ordering[String] {
  def compare(a: String, b: String): Int = a.compareTo(b)
})
```

Just as with Java, to create an anonymous class instance in Scala, you use the new keyword with braces and define the implementation within the body. Notice that you don't need to add the constructor brackets (new Ordering[String]()).

First-class Functions

As we've seen, an anonymous function is called a lambda. It's a compact way to define a function. Anonymous functions are useful when you want to define calculations or transformations and apply them to different values later. For example, passing functions into other functions or storing function definitions for later use.

This kind of usage is referred to as treating functions as *first-class citizens*. Specifically, a language supports first-class functions, if it:

1. Supports passing functions as arguments into other functions.

2. Can return functions as values from other functions.

3. Can store them in variables or within data structures.

> **Higher-Order Functions**
>
> A higher-order function is any function that takes one or more functions as arguments or returns a function. Higher-order functions tend to be more flexible and easier to reuse than the alternative.

Lambdas facilitate first-class function support by providing a compact syntax and by the fact that the compiler generates special bytecode for the lambda syntax.[9]

A lambda defining the preceding sorting calculations looks like this:

```
(String a, String b) -> a.compareTo(b);      // java

(a: String, b: String) => a.compareTo(b)     // scala
```

Passing in Functions

Why would you want to pass a function into a function. Short answer: for flexibility. The sort or sorted functions given earlier are a good example. You can create one function to sort a list but allow the caller to influence how it's sorted.

For example, you can sort the list by ascending or descending order by passing in different function literals.

```
// java
List<String> list = Arrays.asList("A", "C", "B", "D");
list.sort((a, b) -> a.compareTo(b));                    // ascending
list.sort((a, b) -> b.compareTo(a));                    // descending
```

The same is true for Scala:

```
// scala
val list = List("A", "C", "B", "D")
list.sorted((a: String, b: String) => a.compareTo(b))   // ascending
list.sorted((a: String, b: String) => b.compareTo(a))   // descending
```

---

[9]Lambdas are called using the invokedynamic bytecode. It's more efficient than generating new classes and instantiating them as is the case for anonymous classes.

Returning Functions

Returning functions from functions is useful to decouple implementation from behavior. You might want to create factory style functions to be passed around or create calculations but don't have all the values yet.

An example might be that you want to convert currency amounts from US dollars. A simple enough function to write, a function that takes a target currency and dollar amount. However, let's say that you want to call this in lots of places but don't want to pass around the target currency everywhere.

If you create a function to create the function, you can call that just once (when you know the target currency) and pass *it* around instead. It saves you passing around implementation details (in this case the target currency) and so decouples clients from the details.

So rather than the imperative way like this:

```scala
// scala
def dollarTo(currency: String, dollar: Double) = {
  if (currency == "GBP") dollar * 0.76
  else if (currency == "EUR") dollar * 0.83
  else dollar
}
```

...you'd create a higher-order function that takes the target currency but returns a function to be evaluated later. That function would take a currency amount and return the converted amount, as below.

```scala
// scala
def dollarTo(currency: String): Double => Double = {
  if (currency == "GBP") dollar => dollar * 0.76
  else if (currency == "EUR") dollar => dollar * 0.83
  else dollar => dollar
}
```

Then rather than lock yourself into the implementation of the imperative version anywhere you call it — for example, from the `'calculateTicketPrice'` function below):

```scala
// scala
def calculateTicketPrice(targetCurrency: String) = {
  dollarTo(targetCurrency, 199.99)
  // ...
}
```

...you instead pass in a function signature anywhere you want the conversion.

```scala
def calculateTicketPrice(currencyConversion: Double => Double) = {
  currencyConversion(199.99)
  // ...
}
```

You can think of it as an informal interface; *any* function that converts one double to another can be used here. Instead of using the one above, you could pass in a function that calls a web service to get latest FX rates or one that shows historical rates without having to change any client code. Neat.

```scala
calculateTicketPrice(dollarTo("GBP"))
calculateTicketPrice(yahooFxRateFor("GBP"))
calculateTicketPrice(historicalRateFor("GBP"))
```

Storing Functions

The following is an example of a lambda to add two numbers together:

```java
(Integer a, Integer b) -> a + b;        // java
```

If you want to store this as a *value*, you need a type. Under the hood, Java treats lambdas as an instance of a *single method interface* (SAM) and provides suitable interfaces in the `java.util.function` package to do so.

It defines `java.util.function.Function` to represent a single argument function and `java.util.function.BiFunction` for a function with two arguments.

You can therefore assign the lambda like this:

```java
// java
BiFunction<Integer, Integer, Integer> plus = (Integer a, Integer b) -> a+b;
```

The BiFunction defines the two input arguments T and U and return value R. So, the above represents a function with two integer arguments, returning another integer.

```
public interface BiFunction<T, U, R> {
    R apply(T t, U u);
}
```

As the variable declaration includes the type information, Java allows you to drop the repetition in the lambda's arguments:

```
// java
BiFunction<Integer, Integer, Integer> plus = (a, b) -> a + b;
```

To execute or apply the function, you'd use the following syntax:

```
// java
plus.apply(2, 2);                       // 4
plus.apply(plus.apply(2, 2), 2);        // 6
```

The Scala version of the basic lambda is as you'd expect:

```
(a: Int, b: Int) => a + b               // scala
```

Although Scala uses the same trick under the covers to represent a function as a type, in this case scala.Function2[Int, Int, Int] it also allows a more succinct representation. So, although you can write it out long hand like this:

```
val plus: Function2[Int, Int, Int] = (a: Int, b: Int) => a + b   // scala
```

...it's more concise to use the *function type* (Int, Int) => Int:

```
val plus: (Int, Int) => Int = (a: Int, b: Int) => a + b          // scala
```

Again, with the additional type information on the val, you can drop the repetition in the lambda arguments.

```
val plus: (Int, Int) => Int = (a, b) => a + b                    // scala
```

Calling it is more succinct as Scala will automatically call the apply method.

```
// scala
plus(2, 2)              // 4
plus(plus(2, 2), 4)     // 8
```

Function Types

Both Java and Scala support functions as first-class citizens as they support all the preceding points. However, an academically interesting difference is that Java doesn't support *function types* whereas Scala does.

Although you can define a lambda's type using `Function2` in Scala as follows:

```
val f: Function2[String, String, Int] = (a, b) => a.compareTo(b)
```

...you can also define it using a function type.

```
val f: (String, String) => Int = (a, b) => a.compareTo(b)
```

The type declaration to the left of the assignment is known as a *function type*. `(String, String) => Int` is a full *type* in Scala, it declares a function from two string arguments returning an integer. It can be used anywhere an ordinary type declaration can be used; to describe the type of a value, as we've done here, an argument to a function, or a return type.

Functions vs. Methods

In Scala, a `def` can be used as a function or a method. Scala developers often talk about functions and shy away from talking about methods, so what's the difference?

A method `def` will be defined within a Scala class, it will usually refer to instance data within the class. Its nomenclature is firmly in the object-oriented world; methods define behaviors for instance objects.

Function `def`s are defined in Scala *singleton objects* (but, if defined in a class, can be converted into functions under certain conditions). Functions are firmly from the mathematical world, they take inputs and produce outputs. In the functional programming world, they don't define behaviors for instance objects but instead implement independent, repeatable transformations or apply calculations.

The difference between a function and a method then is partly about describing the context of their use; you talk about methods when you're building object-oriented systems and functions when talking about transformations or functional programming. Methods will also be associated with *instance objects* and functions will not.

There are several ways to create functions in Scala.

1. A def in a *singleton object* is inherently a function.

2. Create a lambda.

3. Create a def in a class which Scala will convert to a function when passed to a higher-order function.

There are only two ways to create functions in Java.

1. Create static class method.

2. Create a lambda.

There is special type of lambda called a closure. In both Java and Scala, these are created differently under the hood. They are closer to anonymous classes than functions as a new instance is created when they are defined. You can therefore argue that they are not "functions" in the sense I'm describing here.

Anonymous Class != Anonymous Function

When you create an anonymous class, you "new up" an instance. A function has no instance associated with it and therefore, an instance of an anonymous class can not be called an anonymous function, even though it can be used and passed around like a *first-class citizen*.

Lambdas vs. Closures

A closure is a special type of lambda. It's an anonymous function but it also captures something from its environment when created.

Every closure is a lambda but not all lambdas are closures! To make it more confusing, an anonymous class can also be called a closure when in captures some data.

Let's take a look at an example. Given the following interface Condition:

```java
// java
interface Condition {
    Boolean isSatisfied();
}
```

...an anonymous class might implement Condition to check if some server has shutdown (it calls waitFor to poll continuously until the isRunning method returns false).

```java
// java
void anonymousClass() {
    final Server server = new HttpServer();
    waitFor(new Condition() {
        @Override
        public Boolean isSatisfied() {
            return !server.isRunning();
        }
    });
}
```

The functionally equivalent closure would look like this:

```java
// java
void closure() {
    Server server = new HttpServer();
    waitFor(() -> !server.isRunning());
}
```

In the interest of completeness, the waitFor method might naively be implemented like this:

```java
// java
class WaitFor {
    static void waitFor(Condition condition) throws InterruptedException {
        while (!condition.isSatisfied())
            Thread.sleep(250);
    }
}
```

Both implementations are closures; the former is an anonymous class and a closure, the latter is a lambda and a closure. As we've said, a closure captures its "environment" at runtime. In the anonymous class version, this means copying the value of server into an anonymous instance of Condition. In the lambda, the server variable would also need to be copied into the function at runtime.

As it's a copy, it has to be declared final to ensure that it can not be changed between when it's captured and when it's used. The value at these two points in time could be very different as closures are often used to defer execution until some later point.

Java uses a neat trick whereby, if it can reason that a variable is never updated, it might as well be final, so it treats it as *effectively final* and you don't need to declare it using the final keyword explicitly.

A lambda, on the other hand, doesn't need to copy its environment or capture any terms. This means it can be treated as a genuine function and not an instance of a class.

The same example expressed as a lambda and not a closure would look like this:

```java
// java
void lambda() {
    Server httpServer = new HttpServer();
    waitFor(server -> !server.isRunning(), httpServer);
}

void waitFor(ServerCondition condition, Server server) {
    while (!condition.isSatisfied(server))
        Thread.sleep(250);
}

interface ServerCondition {
    Boolean isSatisfied(Server server);
}
```

The trick here is that the lambda takes the httpServer instance as an argument and so doesn't need to capture it on construction. It doesn't reference anything outside of its scope so nothing is copied in. The same lambda instance can be reused with different instances of a server.

It's an important distinction to make as a lambda doesn't need to be instantiated many times. A closure has to be instantiated and memory allocated for each value it closes over. Memory need only be allocated once for non-closure lambdas and then the lambda can be reused. This makes it more efficient, at least in theory.

Cheat Sheet

If a lambda has no arguments and references something outside of its scope, it's also a closure.

If a lambda works only on things passed in as parameters, it's not a closure.

```
(x) -> x * 2;      // lambda
() -> x * 2;       // closure
```

CHAPTER 11

Inheritance

In this chapter we'll look at inheritance in Scala: how you create subclasses and override methods, the Scala equivalent of interfaces and abstract classes, and the mechanisms Scala offers for mixing in reusable behavior. We'll finish by discussing how to pick between all the options.

Subtype Inheritance

Creating a subtype of another class is the same as in Java. You use the `extends` keyword and you can prevent subclassing with the `final` modifier on a class definition.

Let's suppose we want to extend the basic `Customer` class from earlier and create a special subtype to represent a `DiscountedCustomer`. A shopping basket might belong to the `Customer` super-class, along with methods to add items to the basket and total its value.

```java
// java
public class Customer {

    private final String name;
    private final String address;
    private final ShoppingBasket basket = new ShoppingBasket();

    public Customer(String name, String address) {
        this.name = name;
        this.address = address;
    }

    public void add(Item item) {
        basket.add(item);
    }
}
```

© Toby Weston 2018

T. Weston, *Scala for Java Developers*, https://doi.org/10.1007/978-1-4842-3108-1_11

```java
    public Double total() {
        return basket.value();
    }
}
```

Let's say the `DiscountedCustomer` is entitled to a 10% discount on all purchases. We can extend `Customer`, creating a constructor to match `Customer`, and call super from it. We can then override the `total` method to apply the discount.

```java
// java
public class DiscountedCustomer extends Customer {

    public DiscountedCustomer(String name, String address) {
        super(name, address);
    }

    @Override
    public Double total() {
        return super.total() * 0.90;
    }
}
```

We do exactly the same thing in Scala. Here's the basic `Customer` class:

```scala
// scala
class Customer(val name: String, val address: String) {

  private final val basket: ShoppingBasket = new ShoppingBasket

  def add(item: Item) {
    basket.add(item)
  }

  def total: Double = {
    basket.value
  }
}
```

When it comes to extending `Customer` to `DiscountedCustomer`, there are a few things to consider. First, we'll create the `DiscountedCustomer` class.

class DiscountedCustomer

If we try and extend `Customer` to create `DiscountedCustomer`, we get a compiler error.

class DiscountedCustomer extends Customer   *// compiler error*

We get a compiler error because we need to call the `Customer` constructor with values for its arguments. We had to do the same thing in Java when we called `super` in the new constructor.

Scala has a primary constructor and auxiliary constructors. Auxiliary constructors must be chained to eventually call the primary constructor and in Scala, only the primary constructor can call the super-class constructor. We can add arguments to the primary constructor like this:

class DiscountedCustomer(name: **String**, address: **String**) **extends Customer**

But we can't call `super` directly like we can in Java.

```
class DiscountedCustomer(name: String, address: String) extends Customer {
  super(name, address)                          // compiler error
}
```

In Scala, to call the super-class constructor you pass the arguments from the primary constructor to the super-class. Notice that the arguments to `DiscountedCustomer` aren't set as `val`. They're not fields; instead, they're locally scoped to the primary constructor and passed directly to the super-class, like this:

```
class DiscountedCustomer(name: String, address: String)
    extends Customer(name, address)
```

Finally, we can implement the discounted `total` method in the subclass.

```
override def total: Double = {
  super.total * 0.90
}
```

There are two things to note here: the `override` keyword is required, and to call the super-classes `total` method, we use `super` and a dot, just like in Java.

The override keyword is like the @Override annotation in Java. It allows the compiler to check for mistakes like misspelling the name of the method or providing the wrong arguments. The only real difference between the Java annotation and Scala's is that it's mandatory in Scala when you override non-abstract methods.

Anonymous Classes

You create anonymous subclasses in a similar way to Java.

In the Java version of the ShoppingBasket class, the add method takes an Item interface. So, to add an item to your shopping basket, you could create an anonymous subtype of Item. Here is a program to add two fixed-price items to Joe's shipping basket. Each item is an anonymous subclass of Item. The basket total after discount would be $5.40.

```java
// java
public class ShoppingBasket {

    private final Set<Item> basket = new HashSet<>();

    public void add(Item item) {
        basket.add(item);
    }

    public Double value() {
        return basket.stream().mapToDouble(Item::price).sum();
    }
}

public class AnonymousClass {
    public static void main(String... args) {
        Customer joe = new DiscountedCustomer("Joe", "128 Bullpen Street");
        joe.add(new Item() {
            @Override
            public Double price() {
                return 2.5;
```

```
        }
    });
    joe.add(new Item() {
        @Override
        public Double price() {
            return 3.5;
        }
    });
    System.out.println("Joe's basket will cost $ " + joe.total());
}
}
```

In Scala, it's pretty much the same. You can drop the brackets on the class name when newing up an Item, and the type from the method signature of price. The override keyword in front of the price method is also optional.

```
// scala
object DiscountedCustomer {
  def main(args: Array[String]) {
    val joe = new DiscountedCustomer("Joe", "128 Bullpen Street")
    joe.add(new Item {
      def price = 2.5
    })
    joe.add(new Item {
      def price = 3.5
    })
    println("Joe's basket will cost $ " + joe.total)
  }
}
```

You create anonymous instances of classes, abstract classes, or Scala traits in just the same way.

Interfaces/Traits

Interfaces in Java are similar to traits in Scala. You can use a trait in much the same way as you can use an interface. You can implement specialized behavior in implementing classes, yet still treat them polymorphically in code. However:

- Traits can have default implementations for methods. These are just like Java's virtual extension methods (new in Java 8 and otherwise known as default methods) but there's no equivalent pre-Java 8.

- Traits can also have fields and even default values for these, something which Java interfaces cannot do. Therefore, traits can have both abstract and concrete methods *and* have state.

- A class can implement any number of traits just as a class can implement any number of interfaces, although extending traits with default implementations in Scala is more like mixing in behaviors than traditional interface inheritance in Java.

- There's a cross-over with Java 8 as you can mixin behavior with Java 8, although there are some differences in semantics and how duplicate methods are handled.

In this section, we'll look at these differences in more detail.

In Java, we might create an interface called Readable to read some data and copy it into a character buffer. Each implementation may read something different into the buffer. For example, one might read the content of a web page over HTTP while another might read a file.

```java
// java
public interface Readable {
    public int read(CharBuffer buffer);
}
```

In Scala, the Java interface would become a trait and it would look like this:

```scala
// scala
trait Readable {
  def read(buffer: CharBuffer): Int
}
```

You just use `trait` rather than `class` when you define it. There's no need to declare methods as `abstract`, as any unimplemented methods are automatically abstract.

Implementing the interface in Java uses the `implements` keyword. For example, if we implement a file reader, we might take a `File` object as a constructor argument and override the `read` method to consume the file. The `read` method would return the number of bytes read.

```java
// java
public class FileReader implements Readable {

    private final File file;

    public FileReader(File file) {
        this.file = file;
    }

    @Override
    public int read(CharBuffer buffer) {
        int read = 0;
        // ...
        return read;
    }
}
```

In Scala, you use `extends` just like when you extend regular classes. You're forced to use the `override` keyword when overriding an existing concrete method, but not when you override an abstract method.

```scala
// scala
class FileReader(file: File) extends Readable {
  override def read(buffer: CharBuffer): Int = {    // override optional
    val linesRead: Int = 0
    return linesRead
  }
}
```

In Java, if you want to implement multiple interfaces you append the interface name to the Java class definition, so we could add AutoClosable behavior to our FileReader.

```java
// java
public class FileReader implements Readable, AutoCloseable {

    private final File file;

    public FileReader(File file) {
        this.file = file;
    }

    @Override
    public int read(CharBuffer buffer) {
        int read = 0;
        // ...
            return read;
        }

    @Override
    public void close() throws Exception {
        // close
    }
}
```

In Scala, you use the with keyword to add additional traits. You do this when you want to extend a regular class, abstract class, or trait. Just use extends for the first and then with for any others. However, just like in Java, you can have *only one* super-class.

```scala
// scala
class FileReader(file: File) extends Readable with AutoCloseable {
  def read(buffer: CharBuffer): Int = {
    val linesRead: Int = 0
    // ...
    return linesRead
}

  def close(): Unit = ???
}
```

> **What's The Question?**
>
> The ??? here is actually a method. It's a handy method you can use to say "I don't know yet".
> It throws a runtime exception if you call it, a bit like UnsupportedOperationException in
> Java. It gets things compiling when you really don't know what you need yet.

Methods on Traits

Java 8 introduced default methods where you can create default implementations on
interfaces. You can do the same thing in Scala with a few extra bits besides.

Let's see where Java interfaces might benefit from having default implementations. We
could start by creating a `Sortable` interface to describe any class that can be sorted. More
specifically, any implementations should be able to sort things of the generic type A. This
implies it's only useful for collection classes so we'll make the interface extend `Iterable`
to make that more obvious.

```java
// java
interface Sortable<A> extends Iterable<A> {
    public List<A> sort();
}
```

If lots of classes implement this, many may well want similar sorting behavior. Some will
want finer-grained control over the implementation. With Java 8, we can provide a default
implementation for the common case. We mark the interface method as `default` indicating
that it has a default implementation, then go ahead and provide an implementation.

Below we're taking advantage of the fact that the object is iterable, and copying its contents
into a new `ArrayList`. We can then use the built-in `sort` method on `List`. The `sort` method
takes a lambda to describe the ordering, and we can take a shortcut to reuse an object's
natural ordering if we say the objects to compare must be `Comparable`. With a slight tweak
to the signature to enforce this we can use the comparator's `compareTo` method. It means
that we have to make type A something that is `Comparable`, but it's still in keeping with the
intent of the `Sortable` interface.

```java
// java
public interface Sortable<A extends Comparable> extends Iterable<A> {
    default public List<A> sort() {
        List<A> list = new ArrayList<>();
        for (A elements: this)
            list.add(elements);
        list.sort((first, second) -> first.compareTo(second));
        return list;
    }
}
```

The default keyword here means that the method is no longer abstract and that any subclasses that don't override it will use it by default. To see this, we can create a class, NumbersList extending Sortable, to contain a list of numbers, and use the default sorting behavior to sort these. There's no need to implement the sort method as we're happy to use the default provided.

```java
// java
public class NumbersUsageExample {

    private static class NumberList implements Sortable<Integer> {
        private Integer[] numbers;

        private NumberList(Integer... numbers) {
            this.numbers = numbers;
        }

        @Override
        public Iterator<Integer> iterator() {
            return Arrays.asList(numbers).iterator();
        }
    }

    public static void main(String... args) {
        Sortable<Integer> numbers = new NumberList(1, 34, 65, 23, 0, -1);
        System.out.println(numbers.sort());
    }
}
```

We can apply the same idea to our Customer example and create a Customers class to collect customers. All we have to do is make sure the Customer class is Comparable and we'll be able to sort our list of customers without implementing the sort method ourselves.

```java
// java
// You'll get a compiler error if Customer isn't Comparable
public class Customers implements Sortable<Customer> {
    private final Set<Customer> customers = new HashSet<>();

    public void add(Customer customer) {
        customers.add(customer);
    }

    @Override
    public Iterator<Customer> iterator() {
        return customers.iterator();
    }
}
```

In our Customer class, if we implement Comparable and the compareTo method, the default natural ordering will be alphabetically by name.

```java
// java
public class Customer implements Comparable<Customer> {

    // ...

    @Override
    public int compareTo(Customer other) {
        return name.compareTo(other.name);
    }
}
```

If we add some customers to the list in random order, we can print them sorted by name (as defined in the compareTo method).

```java
// java
public class CustomersUsageExample {
    public static void main(String... args) {
        Customers customers = new Customers();
```

89

```
    customers.add(new Customer("Velma Dinkley", "316 Circle Drive"));
    customers.add(new Customer("Daphne Blake", "101 Easy St"));
    customers.add(new Customer("Fred Jones", "8 Tuna Lane,"));
    customers.add(new DiscountedCustomer("Norville Rogers", "1 Lane"));
    System.out.println(customers.sort());
  }
}
```

In Scala, we can go through the same steps. Firstly, we'll create the basic trait.

```
// scala
trait Sortable[A] {
  def sort: Seq[A]        // no body means abstract
}
```

This creates an abstract method sort. Any extending class has to provide an implementation, but we can provide a default implementation by just providing a regular method body.

```
// scala
trait Sortable[A <: Ordered[A]] extends Iterable[A] {
  def sort: Seq[A] = {
    this.toList.sorted     // built-in sorting method
  }
}
```

We extend Iterable and give the generic type A a constraint that it must be a subtype of Ordered. Ordered is like Comparable in Java and is used with built-in sorting methods. The <: keyword indicates the *upper bound* of A. We're using it here just as we did in the Java example to constrain the generic type to be a subtype of Ordered.

Recreating the Customers collection class in Scala would look like this:

```
// scala
import scala.collections._

class Customers extends Sortable[Customer] {
  private val customers = mutable.Set[Customer]()
  def add(customer: Customer) = customers.add(customer)
  def iterator: Iterator[Customer] = customers.iterator
}
```

We have to make Customer extend Ordered to satisfy the upper-bound constraint, just as we had to make the Java version implement Comparable. Having done that, we inherit the default sorting behavior from the trait.

```scala
// scala
object Customers {
  def main(args: Array[String]) {
    val customers = new Customers()
    customers.add(new Customer("Fred Jones", "8 Tuna Lane,"))
    customers.add(new Customer("Velma Dinkley", "316 Circle Drive"))
    customers.add(new Customer("Daphne Blake", "101 Easy St"))
    customers.add(new DiscountedCustomer("Norville Rogers", "1 Lane"))
    println(customers.sort)
  }
}
```

The beauty of the default method is that we can override it and specialize it if we need to. For example, if we want to create another sortable collection class for our customers but this time sort the customers by the value of their baskets, we can override the sort method.

In Java, we'd create a new class that extends Customers and overrides the default sort method.

```java
// java
public class CustomersSortableBySpend extends Customers {
    @Override
    public List<Customer> sort() {
        List<Customer> customers = new ArrayList<>();
        for (Customer customer: this)
            customers.add(customer);
        customers.sort((first, second) ->
                second.total().compareTo(first.total()));
        return customers;
    }
}
```

The general approach is the same as the default method, but we've used a different implementation for the sorting. We're now sorting based on the total basket value of the customer. In Scala we'd do pretty much the same thing.

```scala
// scala
class CustomersSortableBySpend extends Customers {
  override def sort: List[Customer] = {
    this.toList.sorted(new Ordering[Customer] {
      def compare(a: Customer, b: Customer) = b.total.compare(a.total)
    })
  }
}
```

We extend Customers and override the sort method to provide our alternative implementation. We're using the built-in sort method again, but this time using a different anonymous instance of Ordering; again, comparing the basket values of the customers.

If you want to create an instance of the comparator as a Scala object rather than an anonymous class, we could do something like the following:

```scala
class CustomersSortableBySpend extends Customers {
  override def sort: List[Customer] = {
    this.toList.sorted(BasketTotalDescending)
  }
}
```

```scala
object BasketTotalDescending extends Ordering[Customer] {
  def compare(a: Customer, b: Customer) = b.total.compare(a.total)
}
```

To see this working, we could write a little test program. We can add some customers to our CustomersSortableBySpend, and add some items to their baskets. I'm using the PricedItem class for the items, as it saves us having to create a stub class for each one like we saw before. When we execute it, we should see the customers sorted by basket value rather than customer name.

```scala
// scala
object CustomersUsageExample {
  def main(args: Array[String]) {
    val customers = new CustomersSortableBySpend()

    val fred = new Customer("Fred Jones", "8 Tuna Lane,")
    val velma = new Customer("Velma Dinkley", "316 Circle Drive")
    val daphne = new Customer("Daphne Blake", "101 Easy St")
    val norville = new DiscountedCustomer("Norville Rogers", "1 Lane")

    daphne.add(PricedItem(2.4))
    daphne.add(PricedItem(1.4))
    fred.add(PricedItem(2.75))
    fred.add(PricedItem(2.75))
    norville.add(PricedItem(6.99))
    norville.add(PricedItem(1.50))

    customers.add(fred)
    customers.add(velma)
    customers.add(daphne)
    customers.add(norville)
    println(customers.sort)
  }
}
```

The output would look like this:

```
Norville Rogers $ 7.641
Daphne Blake $ 3.8
Fred Jones $ 2.75
Velma Dinkley $ 0.0
```

Converting Anonymous Classes to Lambdas

In the Java version of the sort method, we could use a lambda to effectively create an instance of Comparable. The syntax is new in Java 8 and in this case, is an alternative to creating an anonymous instance in-line.

```java
// java
customers.sort((first, second) -> second.total().compareTo(first.total()));
```

To make the Scala version more like the Java one, we'd need to pass in a lambda instead of the anonymous instance of Ordering. Scala supports lambdas so we can pass anonymous functions directly into other functions, but the signature of the sort method wants an Ordering, not a function.

Luckily, we can coerce Scala into converting a lambda *into* an instance of Ordering using an *implicit* conversion.[10] All we need to do is create a converting method that takes a lambda or function and returns an Ordering, and mark it as implicit. The implicit keyword tells Scala to try and use this method to convert from one to the other if otherwise things wouldn't compile.

```scala
// scala
implicit def functionToOrdering[A](f: (A, A) => Int): Ordering[A] = {
  new Ordering[A] {
    def compare(a: A, b: A) = f.apply(a, b)
  }
}
```

The signature takes a function and returns an Ordering[A]. The function itself has two arguments and returns an Int. So, our conversion method is expecting a function with two arguments of type A, returning an Int ((A, A) => Int).

Now we can supply a function literal to the sorted method that would otherwise not compile. As long as the function conforms to the (A, A) => Int signature, the compiler will detect that it can be converted to something that does compile and call our implicit method to do so. We can therefore modify the sort method of CustomersSortableBySpend like this:

```scala
// scala
this.toList.sorted((a: Customer, b: Customer) => b.total.compare(a.total))
```

---

[10]Since Scala 2.12, anonymous classes can be converted into Java SAMs automatically.

...passing in a lambda rather than an anonymous class. It's similar to the following equivalent Java version and means we don't need the BasketTotalDescending object anymore.

```java
// java
list.sort((first, second) -> first.compareTo(second));
```

Concrete Fields on Traits

We've looked at default methods on traits, but Scala also allows you to provide default values. You can specify fields in traits.

```scala
// scala
trait Counter {
  var count = 0
  def increment()
}
```

Here, count is a field on the trait. All classes that extend Counter will have their own instance of count copied in. It's not inherited—it's a distinct value *specified* by the trait as being required and supplied for you by the compiler. Subtypes are provided with the field by the compiler and it's initialized (based on the value in the trait) on construction.

For example, count is magically available to the following class and we're able to increment it in the increment method.

```scala
// scala
class IncrementByOne extends Counter {
  override def increment(): Unit = count += 1
}
```

In this example, increment is implemented to multiply the value by some other value on each call.

```scala
// scala
class ExponentialIncrementer(rate: Int) extends Counter {
  def increment(): Unit = if (count == 0) count = 1 else count *= rate
}
```

Incidentally, we can use protected on the var in Counter and it will have similar schematics as protected in Java. It gives visibility to subclasses but, unlike Java, not to other types in the same package. It's slightly more restrictive than Java. For example, if we change it and try to access the count from a non-subtype in the same package, we won't be allowed.

```scala
// scala
trait Counter {
  protected var count = 0
  def increment()
}

class NotASubtype {
  val counter = new IncrementByOne()      // a subtype of Counter but
  counter.count                           // count is now inaccessible
}
```

Abstract Fields on Traits

You can also have abstract values on traits by leaving off the initializing value. This forces subtypes to supply a value.

```scala
// scala
trait Counter {
  protected var count: Int                // abstract
  def increment()
}

class IncrementByOne extends Counter {
  override var count: Int = 0             // forced to supply a value
  override def increment(): Unit = count += 1
}
```

```
class ExponentialIncrementer(rate: Int) extends Counter {
  var count: Int = 1
  def increment(): Unit = if (count == 0) count = 1 else count *= rate
}
```

Notice that IncrementByOne uses the override keyword whereas Exponential Incrementer doesn't. For both fields and abstract methods, override is optional.

Abstract Classes

Vanilla abstract classes are created in Java with the abstract keyword. For example, we could write another version of our Customer class but this time make it abstract. We could also add a single method to calculate the customer's basket value and mark that as abstract.

```
// java
public abstract class AbstractCustomer {
    public abstract Double total();
}
```

In the subclass, we could implement our discounted basket like this:

```
// java
public class DiscountedCustomer extends AbstractCustomer {

    private final ShoppingBasket basket = new ShoppingBasket();

    @Override
    public Double total() {
        return basket.value() * 0.90;
    }
}
```

In Scala, you still use the `abstract` keyword to denote a class that cannot be instantiated. However, you don't need it to qualify a method; you just leave the implementation off.

```scala
// scala
abstract class AbstractCustomer {
  def total: Double        // no implementation means it's abstract
}
```

Then we can create a subclass in the same way we saw earlier. We use `extends` like before and simply provide an implementation for the `total` method. Any method that implements an abstract method doesn't require the `override` keyword in front of the method, although it is permitted.

```scala
// scala
class HeavilyDiscountedCustomer extends AbstractCustomer {
  private final val basket = new ShoppingBasket

  def total: Double = {
    return basket.value * 0.90
  }
}
```

Polymorphism

Where you might use inheritance in Java, there are more options available to you in Scala. Inheritance in Java typically means subtyping classes to inherit behavior *and* state from the super-class. You can also view implementing interfaces as inheritance where you inherit behavior but not state.

In both cases the benefits are around *substitutability*: the idea that you can replace one type with another to change system behavior without changing the structure of the code. This is referred to as inclusion polymorphism.

Scala allows for inclusion polymorphism in the following ways:

- Traits without default implementations.

- Traits with default implementations (because these are used to "mix in" behavior, they're often called mixin traits).

- Abstract classes (with and without fields).

- Traditional class extension.

- Structural types, a kind of duck typing familiar to Ruby developers but which uses reflection.

Traits vs. Abstract Classes

There are a couple of differences between traits and abstract classes. The most obvious is that traits cannot have constructor arguments. Traits also provide a way around the problem of multiple inheritance that you'd see if you were allowed to extend multiple classes directly. Like Java, a Scala class can only have a single super-class, but can mixin as many traits required. So, despite this restriction, Scala does support multiple inheritance. Kind of.

Multiple inheritance can cause problems when subclasses inherit behavior or fields from more than one super-class. In this scenario, with methods defined in multiple places, it's difficult to reason about which implementation should be used. The *is a* relationship breaks down when a type has multiple super-classes.

Scala allows for a kind of multiple inheritance by distinguishing between the class hierarchy and the trait hierarchy. Although you can't extend multiple classes, you can mixin multiple traits. Scala uses a process called linearization to resolve duplicate methods in traits. Specifically, Scala puts all the traits in a line and resolves calls to super by going from right to left along the line.

Does Scala Support Multiple Inheritance?

If by "inheritance" you mean classic class extension, then Scala doesn't support multiple inheritance. Scala allows only a single class to be "extended". It's the same as Java in that respect. However, if you mean can behavior be inherited by other means, then yes, Scala does support multiple inheritance.

A Scala class can mixin behavior from any number of traits, just as Java 8 can mixin behavior from multiple interfaces with default methods. The difference is in how they resolve clashes. Scala uses linearization to predictably resolve a method call at runtime, whereas Java 8 relies on compilation failure.

Linearization means that the order in which traits are defined in a class definition is important (see Figure 11-1). For example, we could have the following:

```
class Animal
trait HasWings extends Animal
trait Bird extends HasWings
trait HasFourLegs extends Animal
```

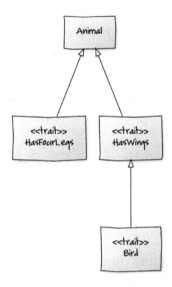

Figure 11-1. *Basic Animal class hierarchy*

If we add a concrete class that extends Animal but also Bird and HasFourLegs, we have a creature (FlyingHorse) that has all of the behaviors in the hierarchy (see Figure 11-2).

```
class Animal
trait HasWings extends Animal
trait Bird extends HasWings
trait HasFourLegs extends Animal
class FlyingHorse extends Animal with Bird with HasFourLegs
```

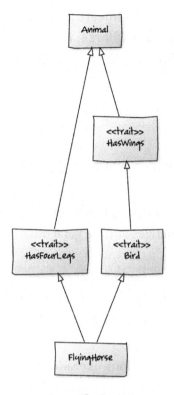

Figure 11-2. *Concrete class* FlyingHorse *extends everything*

The problem comes when we have a method that any of the classes could implement and potentially call that method on their super-class. Let's say there's a method called move. For an animal with legs, move might mean to travel forwards, whereas an animal with wings might travel upwards as well as forwards, as shown in Figure 11-3. If you call move on our FlyingHorse, which implementation would you expect to be called? How about if it in turn calls super.move?

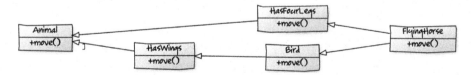

Figure 11-3. *How should a call to move resolve?*

Scala addresses the problem using the linearization technique. Flattening the hierarchy from right to left would give us FlyingHorse, HasForLegs, Bird, HasWings, and finally Animal, (see Figure 11-4). So, if any of the classes call a super-class's method, it will resolve in that order.

Figure 11-4. *Class FlyingHorse extends Animal with Bird with HasFourLegs*

If we change the order of the traits and swap HasFourLegs with Birds, as shown in Figure 11-5, the linearization changes and we get a different evaluation order.

Figure 11-5. *Class FlyingHorse extends Animal with HasFourLegs with Bird*

Figure 11-6 shows what the examples look like side by side.

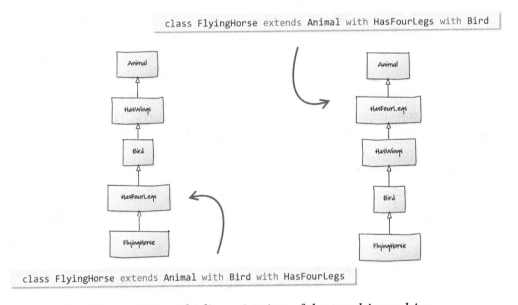

Figure 11-6. *The linearization of the two hierarchies*

With default methods in Java 8 there is no linearization process: any potential clash causes the compiler to error and the programmer has to refactor around it.

Apart from allowing multiple inheritance, traits can also be stacked or layered on top of each other to provide a call chain, similar to aspect-oriented programming, or using decorators. There's a good section on layered traits in *Scala for the Impatient*[11] by Cay S. Horstmann if you want to read more.

Deciding Between the Options

Here are some tips to help you choose when to use the different inheritance options.

Use traits without state when you would have used an interface in Java; namely, when you define a *role* a class should play where different implementations can be swapped in. For example, when you want to use a test double when testing and a "real" implementation in production. "Role" in this sense implies no reusable concrete behavior, just the idea of substitutability.

When your class has behavior and that behavior is likely to be overridden by things of the same type, use a regular class and extend. Both of these are types of inclusion polymorphism.

Use an abstract class in the case when you're more interested in reuse than in an OO *is a* relationship. For example, data structures might be a good place to reuse abstract classes, but our `Customer` hierarchy from earlier might be better implemented as non-abstract classes.

If you're creating reusable behavior that may be reused by unrelated classes, make it a mixin trait as they have fewer restrictions on what can use them compared to abstract classes.

Odersky also talks about some other factors, like performances and Java interoperability, in *Programming in Scala*.[12]

---

[11]http://amzn.to/1yskLc7
[12]http://www.artima.com/pins1ed/traits.html#12.7

CHAPTER 12

Control Structures

This chapter is all about control structures, like `if` statements, switch blocks, loops, and breaks. Specifically, we'll look at the following:

- Conditionals like `if` statements, ternary expressions, and switches.
- Looping structures: `do`, `while` and `for`
- Breaking control flow.
- Exceptions, briefly.

Conditionals

Ifs and Ternaries

Conditionals are straightforward.

```
// java
if (age > 55) {
    retire();
} else {
    carryOnWorking();
}
```

An `if` in Java looks exactly the same in Scala.

```
// scala
if (age > 55) {
  retire()
} else {
  carryOnWorking()
}
```

© Toby Weston 2018
T. Weston, *Scala for Java Developers*, https://doi.org/10.1007/978-1-4842-3108-1_12

You'll often find Scala developers dropping the braces for simple `if` blocks. For example:

```
if (age > 55)
  retire()
else
  carryOnWorking()
```

...or even pulling it all onto one line.

```
if (age > 55) retire() else carryOnWorking()
```

This style is favored because if/else is actually an expression in Scala and not a statement, and the more concise syntax makes it look more like an expression. What's the difference? Well, an expression *returns* a value whereas a statement *carries out* an action.

Expressions vs. Statements

An *expression* returns a value whereas a *statement* carries out an action. Statements by their nature often have side effects whereas expressions are less likely to do so.

For example, let's add a creation method to our `Customer` class that will create either a `DiscountedCustomer` or a regular `Customer` based on how long they've been a customer.

```
// java
public static Customer create(String name, String address,
        Integer yearsOfCustom) {
    if (yearsOfCustom > 2) {
        return new DiscountedCustomer(name, address);
    } else {
        return new Customer(name, address);
    }
}
```

In Java, we're forced to return the new `Customer` from the method. The conditions are statements, things that execute, not expressions that return values. We could do it longhand and create a variable, set then return it, but the point is the same; the statements here have to cause a side effect.

```java
public static Customer create(String name, String address,
        Integer yearsOfCustom) {
    Customer customer = null;
    if (yearsOfCustom > 2) {
        customer = new DiscountedCustomer(name, address);
    } else {
        customer = new Customer(name, address);
    }
    return customer;
}
```

Because conditionals in Scala *are* expressions, you don't need to jump through these hoops. In the Scala equivalent, we can just create the `if` and both branches will return a customer. As the entire expression is the last statement in the method, it is what will be returned from the method.

```scala
// scala
object Customer {
  def create(name: String, address: String, yearsOfCustom: Int) = {
    if (yearsOfCustom > 2)
      new DiscountedCustomer(name, address)
    else
      new Customer(name, address)
  }
}
```

Longhand, we can assign the result of the `if` (remember it's an expression not a statement) to a `val` and then return the value on the last line.

```scala
object Customer {
  def create(name: String, address: String, yearsOfCustom: Int) = {
    val customer = if (yearsOfCustom > 2)
      new DiscountedCustomer(name, address)
```

```scala
    else
      new Customer(name, address)
    customer
  }
}
```

Another trivial example might be something like this:

```scala
val tall = if (height > 190) "tall" else "not tall"      // scala
```

You may have noticed this behaves like a ternary expression in Java.

```java
String tall = height > 190 ? "tall" : "not tall";        // java
```

So, ternaries *are* expressions in Java but `if` statements are not. Scala has no conditional operator (`?:`) because a regular Scala `if` is an expression; it's equivalent to Java's conditional operator. In fact, the bytecode generated for an `if` uses a ternary.

You don't have to use an `if` in Scala like a ternary and assign it to anything, but it's important to realize that it is an expression and has a value. In fact, everything in Scala is an expression. Even a simple block (denoted with curly braces) will return something.

Switch Statements

There are no switch statements as such in Scala. Scala uses *match expressions* instead. These look like they're switching but differ in that the whole thing is an expression and not a statement. So, as we saw with the `if`, Scala's switch-like construct *has a value*. It also uses something called *pattern matching*, which is a lot more powerful as it allows you to select on more than just equality.

In Java, you might write a switch to work out which quarter a particular month falls in. So, January, February, and March are in the first quarter, April, May, and June in the second, and so on.

```java
// java
public class Switch {
    public static void main(String... args) {
        String month = "August";
        String quarter;
```

```
switch (month) {
    case "January":
    case "February":
    case "March":
        quarter = "1st quarter";
        break;
    case "April":
    case "May":
    case "June":
        quarter = "2nd quarter";
        break;
    case "July":
    case "August":
    case "September":
        quarter = "3rd quarter";
        break;
    case "October":
    case "November":
    case "December":
        quarter = "4th quarter";
        break;
    default:
        quarter = "unknown quarter";
        break;
    }
    System.out.println(quarter);
  }
}
```

The break is required to stop the statement execution falling through. When Java selects a case, it has to have a side effect to be useful. In this case, it assigns a value to a variable.

In Scala, we'd start with something like this:

```
// scala
object BrokenSwitch extends App {
  val month = "August"
```

```scala
    var quarter = "???"
    month match {
    case "January"   =>
    case "February"  =>
    case "March"     => quarter = "1st quarter"
    case "April"     =>
    case "May"       =>
    case "June"      => quarter = "2nd quarter"
    case "July"      =>
    case "August"    =>
    case "September" => quarter = "3rd quarter"
    case "October"   =>
    case "November"  =>
    case "December"  => quarter = "4th quarter"
    case _           => quarter = "unknown quarter"
    }
    println(month + " is " + quarter)
  }
```

The above is a direct syntactic translation. However, Scala doesn't support the break keyword so we have to leave that out. Rather than switch we use match and we're saying "does the month *match* any of these case clauses?"

Rather than the colon, we use => and the underscore at the bottom is the catch-all, the same as default in Java. Underscore is often used in Scala to mean an unknown value.

So, although this is a direct translation, when we run it, something has gone wrong. The result hasn't been set.

The output says:

August is ???

Unlike Java, if a case matches, the break is implicit—there is no fall-through to the next case. So, we'll have to add some code to the empty blocks.

```scala
// scala
object Switch extends App {
  val month = "August"
```

```scala
  var quarter = "???"
  month match {
    case "January"   => quarter = "1st quarter"
    case "February"  => quarter = "1st quarter"
    case "March"     => quarter = "1st quarter"
    case "April"     => quarter = "2nd quarter"
    case "May"       => quarter = "2nd quarter"
    case "June"      => quarter = "2nd quarter"
    case "July"      => quarter = "3nd quarter"
    case "August"    => quarter = "3rd quarter"
    case "September" => quarter = "3rd quarter"
    case "October"   => quarter = "4th quarter"
    case "November"  => quarter = "4th quarter"
    case "December"  => quarter = "4th quarter"
    case _           => quarter = "unknown quarter"
  }
  println(month + " is " + quarter)
}
```

This time it works but we've duplicated a fair bit.

To remove some of the duplication, we can combine January, February, and March onto one line, separating them with an or. This means that the month can match either January, February, *or* March. In all of these cases, what follows the => will be executed.

```scala
case "January" | "February" | "March" => quarter = "1st quarter"
```

Doing this for the rest of the cases would give us the following:

```scala
// scala
object SwitchWithLessDuplication extends App {
  val month = "August"
  var quarter = "???"
  month match {
    case "January" | "February" | "March"     => quarter = "1st quarter"
    case "April" | "May" | "June"             => quarter = "2nd quarter"
    case "July" | "August" | "September"      => quarter = "3rd quarter"
    case "October" | "November" | "December"  => quarter = "4th quarter"
```

```scala
    case _ => quarter = "unknown quarter"
  }
  println(month + " is " + quarter)
}
```

We've condensed the preceding code by writing expressions within the case clauses themselves. This becomes more powerful when we think of these case clauses as *patterns* that we can use to build up more and more expressive conditions for the match.

Java can only switch on primitives, enums, and, from Java 7, string values. Thanks to pattern matching, Scala can match on almost anything, including objects. We'll look more at pattern matching in Part III.

The other thing to note is that Scala's version of the switch *is an* expression. We're not forced to work with side effects and can drop the temporary variable and return a String to represent the quarter the month falls into. We can then change the quarter variable from being a var to a val.

```scala
// scala
object SwitchExpression extends App {
  val month = "August"
  val quarter = month match {
    case "January" | "February" | "March"      => "1st quarter"
    case "April" | "May" | "June"              => "2nd quarter"
    case "July" | "August" | "September"       => "3rd quarter"
    case "October" | "November" | "December" => "4th quarter"
    case _ => "unknown quarter"
  }
  println(month + " is " + quarter)
}
```

We could even do it in-line. We just need to add some parentheses around the match, like this:

```scala
// scala
object SwitchExpression extends App {
  val month = "August"
  println(month + " is " + (month match {
    case "January" | "February" | "March"      => "1st quarter"
```

```
    case "April"   | "May"      | "June"                => "2nd quarter"
    case "July"    | "August"   | "September"           => "3rd quarter"
    case "October" | "November" | "December"            => "4th quarter"
    case _
  }))
}
```

Looping Structures: do, while and for

Scala and Java share the same syntax for do and while loops. For example, the following code uses a do and a while to print the numbers zero to nine:

```
// java
int i = 0;
do {
    System.out.println(i);
    i++;
} while (i < 10);
```

The Scala version would look like this (there is no ++ incrementer so we use += instead):

```
// scala
var i: Int = 0
do {
  println(i)
  i += 1
} while (i < 10)
```

And while loops are the same.

```
// java
int i = 0;
while (i < 10) {
    System.out.println(i);
    i++;
}
```

```scala
// scala
var i: Int = 0
while (i < 10) {
  println(i)
  i += 1
}
```

Things get more interesting when we look at for loops. Scala doesn't have for loops like Java does; it has what's referred to as the "generator-based for loop" and the related "for comprehension" instead. To all intents and purposes, these can be used like Java's for loop construct, so for the most part you won't have to worry about the technical differences.

Java's for loop controls the iteration in three stages, as shown in Figure 12-1: initialize, check, and update.

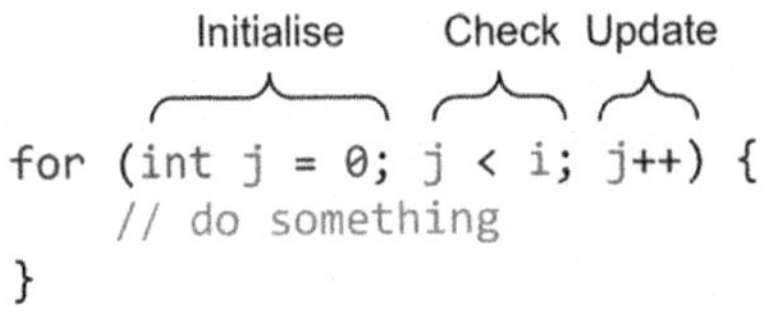

Figure 12-1. The typical for loop iteration stages

There is no direct analog in Scala. You've seen an alternative—using the while loop to initialize a variable, check a condition, then update the variable—but you can also use a generator-based for loop in Scala. So, the following for in Java:

```java
// java
for (int i = 0; i < 10; i++) {
    System.out.println(i);
}
```

...would look like this using a generator-based for loop in Scala:

```scala
// scala
for (i <- 0 to 9) {
  println(i)
}
```

The i variable has been created for us and is assigned a value on each iteration. The arrow indicates that what follows is a *generator*. A generator is something that can feed values into the loop. The whole thing is a lot like Java's enhanced for loops where anything that is Iterable can be used. In the same way, anything that can generate an iteration in Scala can be used as a generator.

In this case, 0 to 9 is the generator. 0 is an Int literal and the class Int has a method called to that takes an Int and returns a range of numbers that can be enumerated. The example uses the infix shorthand, but we could have written it longhand like this:

```
for (i <- 0.to(9)) {
  println(i)
}
```

It's very similar to the following enhanced for loop in Java, using a list of numbers:

```
// java
List<Integer> numbers = Arrays.asList(0, 1, 2, 3, 4, 5, 6, 7, 8, 9);
for (Integer i : numbers) {
    System.out.println(i);
}
```

...which itself could be rewritten in Java as the following:

```
numbers.forEach(i -> System.out.println(i));              // java
```

...or as a method reference.

```
numbers.forEach(System.out::println);                     // java
```

Unsurprisingly, Scala has a foreach method of its own.

```
(0 to 9).foreach(i => println(i))                         // scala
```

We use the to method again to create a sequence of numbers. This sequence has the foreach method, which we call, passing in a lambda. The lambda function takes an Int and returns Unit.

We can even use Scala's shorthand like we did with Java's method reference as follows:

```
(0 to 10).foreach(println(_))                             // scala
```

115

> **For Loop vs. For Comprehension**
>
> What's the difference between the generator-based for loop and the for comprehension?
>
> The generator-based for loop will be converted by the compiler into a call to `foreach` against the collection. A for comprehension will be converted to a call to `map` on the collection. The for comprehension adds the keyword `yield` to the syntax.
>
> **for** (i **<-** 0 to 5) **yield** i * 2   *// results in (0, 2, 4, 6, 8, 10)*
>
> See Chapter 19, For Comprehensions, for more details.

Breaking Control Flow (**break** and **continue**)

Scala has no break or continue statements, and generally discourages you from breaking out of loops. However, you can use a library method to achieve the same thing. In Java, you might write something like this to break out of a loop early:

```java
// java
for (int i = 0; i < 100; i++) {
    System.out.println(i);
    if (i == 10)
        break;
}
```

In Scala, you need to import a Scala library class called Breaks. You can then enclose the code to break out from in a "breakable" block and call the break method to break out. It's implemented by throwing an exception and catching it.

```scala
// scala
import scala.util.control.Breaks._
breakable {                              // breakable block
  for (i <- 0 to 100) {
    println(i)
    if (i == 10)
      break()                            // break out of the loop
  }
}
```

Exceptions

Exceptions in Scala are handled in the same way as Java. They have all the same schematics in terms of interrupting control flow and aborting the program if not dealt with.

Exceptions in Scala extend `java.lang.Throwable` like their Java counterparts but Scala has no concept of checked exceptions. All checked exceptions thrown from existing Java libraries get converted to `RuntimeExceptions`. Any exceptions you throw don't need to be dealt with to keep the compiler happy; all exceptions in Scala are runtime exceptions (see Figure 12-2).

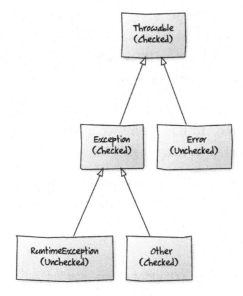

Figure 12-2. *The Java exception hierarchy. Scala doesn't use checked exceptions.*

Catching exceptions uses pattern matching like we saw earlier with match expressions. In Java you might do something like this to get the contents of a web page:

```
// java
try {
    URL url = new URL("http://baddotrobot.com");
    BufferedReader reader = new BufferedReader(
        new InputStreamReader(url.openStream()));
    try {
        String line;
```

```java
      while ((line = reader.readLine()) != null)
          System.out.println(line);
    } finally {
        reader.close();
    }
  } catch (MalformedURLException e) {
      System.out.println("Bad URL");
  } catch (IOException e) {
      System.out.println("Problem reading data: " + e.getMessage());
  }
```

We start with a URL to attempt to download. This can throw a `Malformed URLException`. As it's a checked exception, we're forced to deal with it. We then create a Reader and open a stream from the URL ready for reading. This can throw another exception, so we're forced to deal with that too.

When we start reading, the `readLine` method can also throw an exception but that's handled by the existing catch. To make sure we clean up properly in the event of an exception here, we close the reader in a `finally` block.

If we want to use Java 7's try-with-resources construct, we can avoid the `finally` clause. The try-with-resources syntax will automatically call `close` on the reader.

```java
// java
try {
    URL url = new URL("http://baddotrobot.com");
    try (BufferedReader reader = new BufferedReader(
            new InputStreamReader(url.openStream()))) {
        String line;
        while ((line = reader.readLine()) != null)
            System.out.println(line);
        }
} catch (MalformedURLException e) {
    System.out.println("Bad URL");
} catch (IOException e) {
    System.out.println("Problem reading data: " + e.getMessage());
}
```

In Scala things look pretty much the same.

```scala
// scala
try {
  val url = new URL("http://baddotrobot.com")
  val reader = new BufferedReader(new InputStreamReader(url.openStream))
  try {
    var line = reader.readLine
    while (line != null) {
      line = reader.readLine
      println(line)
    }
  } finally {
    reader.close()
  }
} catch {
  case e: MalformedURLException => println("Bad URL")
  case e: IOException => println(e.getMessage)
}
```

We create the URL as before. Although it can throw an exception, we're not forced to catch it. It's a Java checked exception but Scala is converting it to a runtime exception.

Although we're not forced to, we do actually want to deal with the exceptions. So, we use the familiar try and catch statements. In the catch, the exceptions are dealt with using match expressions. We can tweak the pattern if we don't actually need the exception in the code block by replacing the variable name with an underscore. This means we don't care about the variable, only the class.

```scala
case _: MalformedURLException => println("Bad URL")
```

We just need to add the finally block back in. finally is just as it is in Java. There is no try-with-resources equivalent in Scala, although you can write your own method to achieve the same thing. (Hint: With something like the Loan pattern.)

CHAPTER 13

Generics

In this chapter we'll look at generics or *type parameterization* or generic programming in Scala. We'll look at the following:

- Syntax for generics: defining types and methods.

- Bounded types, extends and super.

- Wildcards in both Java and Scala.

- Covariance and contravariance.

Parametric Polymorphism

We talked briefly about subtype or *inclusion* polymorphism; the idea that subtypes can be substituted to stand in for their super-types. These stand-ins can provide different behavior without changing the structure of your code. The types of polymorphism are:

- Inclusion polymorphism (see Chapter 11, Inheritance).

- Ad hoc polymorphism (which is basically method overloading).

- Parametric polymorphism.

Parametric polymorphism allows us to write code generically without depending on specific types, yet still maintain type safety. We use it all the time when we work with classes that work against multiple types. For example:

```
List<Customer> customers = new ArrayList<>();      // java
```

© Toby Weston 2018
T. Weston, *Scala for Java Developers*, https://doi.org/10.1007/978-1-4842-3108-1_13

Parametric polymorphism will be familiar if you've ever created a list of something in Java. It's more commonly referred to as generics; by giving a generic type (like `List`) a parameterized type, we can treat it as a list yet still refer to its contents in a type-safe way. Generics are at play even if you don't specify the parameterized type in Java. So, although you can write the following:

```
List collection = new ArrayList();                // java
```

...you're actually creating a generic `List` of type `Object`.

```
List<Object> collection = new ArrayList<>();      // java
```

Diamond Operator

You can create a list of Object in Java like this:

```
List<Object> collection = new ArrayList<>();
```

The diamond operator (`<>`) on the right-hand side of the assignment was new in Java 7, you were forced to repeat the generic type declaration on the right-hand side.

Class Generics

When you create a list of a specific type, Java will give you type safety on `List` methods that take parameters and return things of that type. For example, creating a list of customers but then trying to add an object that isn't a customer will result in a compiler failure.

```
List<Customer> customers = new ArrayList<>();
customers.add(new HockeyPuck());                  // compiler failure
```

The basic syntax for Scala will look familiar to Java developers; we just replace the chevrons with square brackets.

```
List<Customer> customers = new ArrayList<>();     // java
```

versus

```scala
val customers: List[Customer] = List()          // scala
```

Creating a list in Scala like this also shows that it has the equivalent of the diamond operator. Scala's type inference can work out that customers is of type Customer without repeating the generics on the right-hand side.

```scala
val customers: List[Customer] = List[Customer]()
                                        ^
                    // no need to repeat the type
```

Method Generics

You can define generic parameters for methods in a similar way. To define a generic parameter to a method without defining a generic type for the whole class, you'd do something like this in Java, where the generic type is defined straight after the public keyword and used as the type of the parameter a.

```java
public <A> void add(A a)              // java
```

...versus this in Scala:

```scala
def add[A](a: A)                      // scala
```

Stack Example

As a slightly more expanded example, in Java, we could generalize a Stack class. We could create an interface Stack with a generic type T and ensure that the push method takes a T and the pop method returns a T.

```java
// java
public interface Stack<T> {
    void push(T t);
    T pop();
}
```

In Scala

```scala
// scala
trait Stack[T] {
  def push(t: T)
  def pop: T
}
```

For demonstration purposes, we could implement Stack using a list in Java like this:

```java
// java
public class ListStack<T> implements Stack<T> {

    private final List<T> elements = new ArrayList<>();

    @Override
    public void push(T t) {
        elements.add(0, t);
    }

    @Override
    public T pop() {
        if (elements.isEmpty())
            throw new IndexOutOfBoundsException();
        return elements.remove(0);
    }
}
```

We "bind" a concrete type to the generic type when we supply the compiler with a concrete type. Adding String to the following declaration (on line 3) "binds" what was the generic type T to String. The compiler knows to replace T with String and we can start using strings as arguments and return types. If we try to add a number to the stack in our example, we'd get a compiler error.

```java
1   // java
2   public static void main(String... args) {
3       Stack<String> stack = new ListStack<>();
4       stack.push("C");
```

```
5        stack.push("B");
6        stack.push("A");
7        stack.push(12);                          // compilation failure
8        String element = stack.pop();
9    }
```

Creating the ListStack in Scala is straightforward. It would look something like this:

```scala
// scala
class ListStack[T] extends Stack[T] {

  private var elements: List[T] = List()

  override def push(t: T): Unit = {
    elements = t +: elements
  }

  override def pop: T = {
    if (elements.isEmpty) throw new IndexOutOfBoundsException
    val head = elements.head
    elements = elements.tail
    head
  }
}
```

We still use a List to store the elements but because Scala's List is immutable, in the push method, we replace the instance with a new list with the element prepended.

Similarly, when we pop, we have to replace the elements with all but the first element using the tail method. We get and return the first element using the head method. You'll come across the idea of head (the first) and tail (the remainder) a lot in Scala and functional programming.

Binding to a concrete type is just the same. In the following example, I'm not declaring the stack variable with a type, so we need to give the compiler a hint about what kind of List it will be by adding the parameterized type on line 3.

```scala
// scala
def main(args: String*) {
    val stack = new ListStack[String]
```

```
4        stack.push("C")
5        stack.push("B")
6        stack.push("A")
7        val element: String = stack.pop
8    }
```

To demonstrate method-level generics, we could add a method to convert a Stack to an array. The thing to note here is that the generic is defined solely in terms of the method. A isn't related to the generic type on the class definition.

```java
// java
public interface Stack<T> {
    static <A> A[] toArray(Stack<A> stack) {
        throw new UnsupportedOperationException();
    }
}
```

You define method-level generics in Scala in just the same way. Below, A is defined purely in scope for the method.

```scala
// scala
object Stack {
  def toArray[A](a: Stack[A]): Array[A] = {
    ???
  }
}
```

Bounded Classes

Let's go back to the list example with a generic type of Customer.

```java
List<Customer> customers = new ArrayList<>();          // java
```

The contents of the list can be any Customer or subtype of Customer, so we can add a DiscountedCustomer to the list.

```java
List<Customer> customers = new ArrayList<>();
customers.add(new Customer("Bob Crispin", "15 Fleetwood Mack Road"));
customers.add(new DiscountedCustomer("Derick Jonar", "23 Woodland Way"));
```

Type erasure sees the collection as containing only Objects. The compiler will ensure that only things of the correct type go into the collection and use a cast on the way out. That means that anything you take out of our example can only be treated as a Customer.

If all you've done is override Customer behavior in the DiscountedCustomer, you can treat the objects polymorphically and you wouldn't see a problem. If you've added methods to DiscountedCustomer, however, you can't call them without an unchecked cast.

```java
for (Customer customer : customers) { // some may be DiscountedCustomers
    // total will be the discounted total for any DiscountedCustomers
    System.out.println(customer.getName() + " : " + customer.total());
}

DiscountedCustomer customer = (DiscountedCustomer) customers.get(0);
System.out.println(customer.getDiscountAmount());
```

To get around this limitation, you can force generic types to be bound to specific types within a class hierarchy. These are called *bounded types*.

Upper Bounds (<U extends T>)

You can restrict a generic type using extends or super in Java. These set the bounds of that type to either be a subtype or super-type. You use extends to set the upper bounds and super, the lower bounds. They can refer to a class or an interface.

We've actually already seen an example of setting an upper bound in the Sortable interface we wrote back in Chapter 11, Inheritance. We created an interface describing generically that things can be sortable.

```java
// java
public interface Sortable<A extends Comparable<A>> extends Iterable<A> {
    default public List<A> sort() {
        List<A> list = new ArrayList<>();
        for (A elements: this)
            list.add(elements);
        list.sort((first, second) -> first.compareTo(second));
        return list;
    }
    // etc
}
```

This does a couple of things with generics. It both defines a generic type A, which must be a subclass of Comparable, and also says that implementing classes must be able to iterate over A. Comparable is the upper bound of A.

This is a good example of why bounded types are useful; because we want to define a general-purpose algorithm yet constrain the types enough that we can call known methods in that algorithm. In the example, we can't implement the sort method unless the class has the compareTo method from Comparable and also is iterable.

We bind the type parameter when we implement the interface.

```java
public class Customers implements Sortable<Customer> { ... }      // java
```

It's at this point that the compiler can start treating A as a Customer and check that Customer implements Comparable and that Customers implements Iterable.

In Scala, it would look like this:

```scala
// scala
trait Sortable[A <: Ordered[A]] extends Iterable[A] {
  def sort: Seq[A] = {
    this.toList.sorted
  }
}

class Customers extends Sortable[Customer] { ... }
```

The upper bound tells you what you can *get out* of a data structure. In our example, the sorting algorithm needed to get something out and use it as a Comparable; it enforces type safety. It's set using extends in Java and <: in Scala.

Lower Bounds (<U super T>)

Setting a lower bound means using the super keyword in Java, something like the following:

```java
public class Example<T, U super T> { }                    // java
```

It's saying that U has to be a super-type of T. It's useful when we want to be flexible in our API design; you'll see it a lot in Java library code or in libraries like Hamcrest. For example, suppose we have a class hierarchy to represent animals.

```java
// java
static class Animal {}
static class Lion extends Animal {}
static class Zebra extends Animal {}
```

We might want to collect the lions together in an enclosure.

```java
// java
List<Lion> enclosure = new ArrayList<>();
enclosure.add(new Lion());
enclosure.add(new Lion());
```

Let's say that we want to sort the lions, and that we already have a helper method, similar to the Sortable interface, that sorts anything that is Comparable.

```java
// java
public static <A extends Comparable<A>> void sort(List<A> list) {
    Collections.sort(list);
}
```

To sort our lions, we just make them comparable and call the sort method.

```java
// java
static class Lion extends Animal implements Comparable<Lion> {
    @Override
    public int compareTo(Lion other) {
        return this.age.compareTo(other.age);
    }
}
sort(enclosure);
```

Great, but what if we expand our enclosure and create a zoo? Notice that the List is now of type Animal rather than Lion.

```java
// java
List<Animal> zoo = new ArrayList<>();
zoo.add(new Lion());
zoo.add(new Lion());
zoo.add(new Zebra());
sort(zoo);                      // compilation error
```

It won't compile, as we can't compare zebras and lions. We need to make the comparison on super-type rather than the subtypes. So, we need to move the implementation of Comparable from Lion to Animal. That way, we can compare zebras to lions and presumably keep them away from each other.

If we make the Lion and Zebra Comparable with Animal, in theory we should be able to compare them with each other and themselves. However, if we move the comparable implementation up to the super-type (that is, Animal implements Comparable and remove it from Lion), like this:

```java
// java
static class Animal implements Comparable<Animal> {
    @Override
    public int compareTo(Animal o) {
        return 0;
    }
}
static class Lion extends Animal { }
static class Zebra extends Animal { }

List<Lion> enclosure = new ArrayList<>();
enclosure.add(new Lion());
enclosure.add(new Lion());
enclosure.sort();                   // compiler failure

List<Animal> zoo = new ArrayList<>();
zoo.add(new Lion());
zoo.add(new Lion());
zoo.add(new Zebra());
sort(zoo);                          // compiles ok now
```

...we get a compiler error when recompiling the original enclosure of Lions. We can no longer sort the Lions enclosure.

```
java: method sort in class Zoo cannot be applied to given types;
    required: java.util.List<A>
    found: java.util.List<Lion>
    reason: inferred type does not conform to equality constraint(s)
```

```
inferred: Animal
equality constraints(s): Lion
```

Otherwise known as:

```
Inferred type 'Lion' for type parameter 'A' is not within its bounds;
  should implement 'Lion'
```

This is because the sort method (public static <A extends Comparable<A>> void sort(List<A> list)) expects a type that is comparable to itself, and we're trying to compare it to something higher up the class hierarchy. When A is bound to a concrete type, for example Lion, Lion must also be Comparable against Lion. The problem is that we've just made it comparable to Animal.

```
static class Lion extends Animal implements Comparable<Animal> { }
```

The zoo (a List<Animal>) can be sorted because the generic type of the collection is Animal.

We can fix it by adding ? super A to the signature of sort. This means that whilst A is still bound to a concrete type, say Lion, we're now saying that it needs to be comparable to some super-type of Lion. As Animal is a super-type of Lion, it conforms and the whole thing compiles again.

```
public static <A extends Comparable<? super A>> void sort(List<A> list) { }
```

The upshot to all this is that our API method sort is much more flexible with a lower bound; without it, we wouldn't be able to sort different types of animal.

In Scala, we can go through the same steps and create the Animal hierarchy.

```scala
// scala
class Animal extends Comparable[Animal] {
  def compareTo(o: Animal): Int = 0
}
class Lion extends Animal
class Zebra extends Animal
```

Then we can create our sort method again and recreate our enclosure.

```scala
// scala
def sort[A <: Comparable[A]](list: List[A]) = { }
```

```scala
// scala
def main(args: String*) {
  var enclosure = List[Lion]()
  enclosure = new Lion +: enclosure
  enclosure = new Lion +: enclosure
  sort(enclosure)                              // compiler failure

  var zoo = List[Animal]()
  zoo = new Zebra +: zoo
  zoo = new Lion +: zoo
  zoo = new Lion +: zoo
  sort(zoo)                                    // compiles OK
}
```

Like before, we get a compilation failure.

```
Error:(30, 5) inferred type arguments [Lion] do not conform to method
  sort's type parameter bounds [A <: Comparable[A]] sort(enclosure)
                                                          ^
```

It correctly enforces that A must be of the same type but we're treating A as both Lion and Animal. So just like before, we need to constrain the generic type with a lower bound.

You might be tempted to try a direct equivalent: using an underscore with >: A:

```scala
def sort[A <: Comparable[_ >: A]](a: List[A]) = { } // compiler failure
```

But unfortunately, this would cause a compilation failure:

```
failure: illegal cyclic reference involving type A
```

It can't cope with the reference to A; it sees it as cyclic. So, you have to try and keep the relationship with the bounds but remove the cyclic reference. The answer is to define a new generic type U and write something like this:

```scala
def sort[A <: Comparable[U], U >: A](list: List[A]) = { }
```

So, A must extend Comparable where the Comparable's generic type U must itself be a super-type of A. This gets rid of the cyclic problem, but the compiler would still complain.

```
inferred type arguments [Lion,Lion] do not conform to method sort's
   type parameter bounds [A <: Comparable[U], U >: A] sort(enclosure)
                                                          ^
```

It's saying that the inferred types for the enclosure don't match the constraints we've set. It has inferred the two types to both be Lion because the inference engine just doesn't have enough to go on. We can give it a hint if we specify the types *we* know to be true. So just like a type witness in Java, we can clarify that we want the types to be Lion and Animal.

```
var enclosure = List[Lion]()
enclosure = new Lion +: enclosure
enclosure = new Lion +: enclosure
sort[Lion, Animal](enclosure)                    // add a type hint
```

When you round-trip the byte code, the final version looks like this:

```
// java
public <T extends Comparable<U>, U> void sort(List<U> a) { }
```

Which is pretty much equivalent to the following:

```
// java
public <T extends Comparable<?>> void sort(List<T> a) { }
```

Which is pretty much the same as the Scala version:

```
def sort[A <: Comparable[_]](list: List[A]) { }    // scala
```

So, it treats it like an unbounded type under the covers. That's not quite true, in the sense that the Scala compiler is doing all the hard work here and leaves U unbounded because it's doing all the type checking. In this example, it doesn't make complete sense to round-trip from byte code to Java, as it's not like-for-like, but it's interesting to see what's going on behind the scenes.

A lower bound tells you what you can *put in* a data structure. In our Lion example, using a lower bound means you can put more than just lions in the zoo. You use super in Java and greater than colon (>:) in Scala.

Wildcard Bounds (<? extends T, <? super T>)

We've already seen some examples of wildcards: the ? in Java and the _ in Scala.

Wildcards with an upper bound look like this:

```java
// java
void printAnimals(List<? extends Animal> animals) {
    for (Animal animal : animals) {
        System.out.println(animal);
    }
}
```

```scala
// scala
def printAnimals(animals: List[_ <: Animal]) {
  for (animal <- animals) {
    println(animal)
  }
}
```

Wildcards with a lower bound look like this:

```java
// java
static void addNumbers(List<? super Integer> numbers) {
    for (int i = 0; i < 100; i++) {
        numbers.add(i);
    }
}
```

```scala
// scala
def addNumbers(numbers: List[_ >: Int]) {
  for (i <- 0 to 99) {
    // ...
  }
}
```

Unbounded wildcards look like this in Java:

```java
List<?> list                 // java
```

...and like this in Scala:

```scala
List[_]                    // scala
```

An unbounded wildcard refers to an unknown generic type. For example, printing elements of a list of unknown type will work with all lists. Just add upper- or lower-bound constraints to limit the options.

```java
// java
void printUnknown(List<?> list) {
    for (Object element : list) {
        System.out.println(element);
    }
}
```

```scala
// scala
def printUnknown(list: List[_]) {
  for (e <- list) {
    val f: Any = e
    println(f)
  }
}
```

Although the implementation can treat the elements as Object because everything is an object, you can't add anything to a list of unknown type.

```java
// java
List<?> list = new ArrayList<String>();
list.add(new Object()); // compiler error
```

The one exception is null.

```java
list.add(null);
```

You get the same effect in Scala, where you can't even create a list without a valid type.

```scala
scala> val list = mutable.MutableList[_]()
<console>:7: error: unbound wildcard type
       val list = mutable.MutableList[_]()
                  ^
```

You mainly use wildcards when you really don't care about the type parameter, just any constraints on an upper or lower bounding, or when you can treat the type as an instance of Object or Any.

Multiple Bounds

Types can also have multiple bounds in both Java and Scala.

- Java is limited to multiple upper bounds.

- Java can't set a lower *and* upper bound on types (so you can't have a generic type extend one thing and also be a super-type to another).

- Scala can set a single lower *and* an upper bound, unlike Java.

- However, Scala can't set multiple upper or lower bounds. Instead it can constrain bounds by also forcing you to extend traits.

Using multiple bounds, another way to express the constraints on the Animal sorting method would be to explicitly state that A must extend Animal *and* be comparable to Animal, using the & symbol in Java.

```
// java
public static <A extends Animal & Comparable<Animal>> void sort(List<A> l)
```

This sets two upper bounds to the generic type A in Java. You can't set two upper bounds on A in Scala, but you can achieve the same effect by specifying that your bound must also extend certain traits.

```
// scala
def sort[A <: Animal with Comparable[Animal]](list: List[A]) = { }
```

Because we're being more explicit, we can remove the type hints when calling the sort method. In fact, you'll get a compiler error if you don't.

```
var enclosure = List[Lion]()
enclosure = new Lion +: enclosure
enclosure = new Lion +: enclosure
// sort[Lion, Animal](enclosure)      // compiler error
sort(enclosure)
```

In Scala, you can also set both a lower and upper bound using >: and <:, like this:

```scala
def example[A >: Lion <: Animal](a: A) = ()            // scala
              ^              ^
            lower       upper
```

...where A must be a super-type of Lion and a subtype of Animal.

Variance

Without involving generics, a simple class B that extends A (see Figure 13-1) can be assigned to an instance of A; it is after all, an A as well as a B. Obviously, subtyping is only in one direction; the other way around, and you get a compiler failure.

```java
// java
A a = new A();
B b = new B();
a = b;
b = a;                      // compiler failure
```

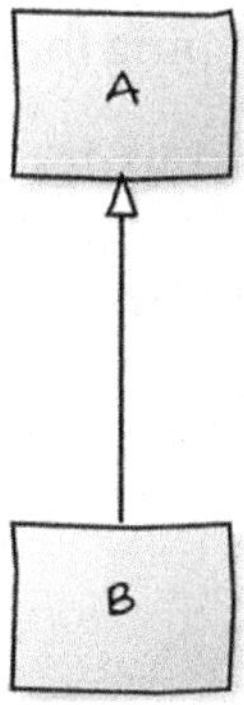

Figure 13-1. B extends A

Generic classes, however, are not subclasses themselves just because their parameterized type may be. So, if B is a subclass of A, should List<B> be a subclass of List<A>? In Java List of B is not a subtype of List of A even though their parameterized types are (see Figure 13-2).

```java
// java
List<B> a = new ArrayList<>();
List<A> b = new ArrayList<>();

a = b; // compiler failure
```

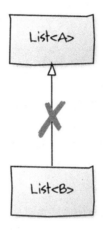

Figure 13-2. *List<B> cannot extend List<A> in Java*

This is where variance comes in. Variance describes how subtyping generic types (like lists or "container" types) relates to subtyping their parameterized type.

There are three types of subtype relationship described by variance.

1. Invariant.

2. Covariant.

3. Contravariant.

Invariance

Java only supports one of the three for its generic types: all generic types in Java are *invariant,* which is why we can't assign a List<B> to a List<A>. Invariant generic types don't preserve the subtype relationship of their parameterized types.

However, you can vary the parameterized types when you use wildcards with methods and variables.

The invariant relationship between generic types says that there is no relationship even if their contents have a subtype relationship. You can't substitute one for another. Java and

Scala share syntax here, as defining any generic type in chevrons (Java) or square brackets (Scala) describes the type as invariant.

```
public class List<T> { }          // java
class List[T] { }                 // scala
```

Covariance

Covariant generic types preserve the relationship between two generic types as subtypes when their parameterized types are subtypes. So, List<B> *is a* subtype of List<A> when a generic type is set up as covariant. Java doesn't support covariance of types. Scala supports covariant generic types by using a + when you define a generic class.

```
class List[+T] { }
```

Contravariance

Contravariance reverses a subtype relationship. So, if A is contravariant, List<A> is also a List<B>; it's a subtype. The relationships of the parameterized types are reversed for their generic types. Java doesn't support contravariance of types but in Scala you just add a - to the generic type definition.

```
class List[-T] { }
```

Variance Summary

In summary, invariant generic types are not related, regardless of the relationship of their parameterized types. Covariant types maintain the subtype relationship of their parameterized types, and contravariant types reverse it (see Table 13-1).

Table 13-1. *Variance summary*

	Description	Scala Syntax
Invariant	List<A> and List<B> are not related	[T]
Covariant	List<B> is a subclass of List<A>	[+T]
Contravariant	List<A> is a subclass of List<B>	[-T]

The syntax for each is summarized in Table 13-2.

Table 13-2. *Syntax summary*

	Invariant	**Covariant**	**Contravariance**
Java	<T>	<? extends T>	<? super T>
Scala	[T]	[+T]	[-T]
Scala (wildcards)	[T]	[_ <: T]	[_ >: T]

Java Limitations

In Java all generic types are invariant, which means you can't assign a List<Foo> to a List<Object>. You *can* vary the types where you use them with wildcards, but only for methods and variable definitions, not classes.

PART III

Beyond Java to Scala

This part of the book is all about the differences between Scala and Java. There are plenty of language features in Scala that don't have an obvious analog in Java. In this part, we'll take a closer look at some of those and explore what Scala can give us over Java.

Specifically, we'll explore a number of the language features that make writing Scala more expressive and we'll look at some of the more functional programming idioms that Scala is so well know for.

Expressive Scala

Scala offers several features that make writing code more concise. As well as some we've already seen, it provides mechanisms to:

- Make methods look like functions using the special case `apply` method.

- Provide default behavior for the assignment operator using a special case `update` method.

- Make regular method calls look like language structures, which in effect means you can define your own control structures.

Scala also offers pattern matching; we'll look at the `unapply` method and its role in pattern matching.

Functional Programming Idioms

We'll also look at some of functional programming aspects of Scala.

- Built-in methods for mapping values (`map`, `flatMap`).

- What monads are and why you should care.

- The `Option` class as a way of avoiding null checks.

- Chaining monad calls.

- For comprehensions and how they work under the hood.

This only scratches the surface of functional programming but I hope that this part of the book will give you a useful head start when it comes to Scala and functional programming.

CHAPTER 14

Faking Function Calls

Scala provides mechanisms to make method calls look like regular function calls. It uses special case `apply` and `update` methods to allow a kind of shorthand call notation that can reduce the clutter of your code.

The `apply` Method

The `apply` method provides a shorthand way of calling a method on a class. So, as we saw, you can use them as factory-style creation methods, where given some class, such as our old friend `Customer`:

```
class Customer(name: String, address: String)
```

...you can add an `apply` method to its companion object.

```
object Customer {
  def apply(name: String, address: String) = new Customer(name, address)
}
```

You can then either call the method directly, or drop the `apply` part, at which point Scala will look for an apply method that matches your argument list and call it.

```
Customer.apply("Bob Fossil", "1 London Road")
Customer("Rob Randal", "14 The Arches")
```

You can also have multiple apply methods. For example, we could create another method to default the address field of our customer.

```
def apply(name: String) = new Customer(name, "No known address")

Customer("Cuthbert Colbert")
```

© Toby Weston 2018
T. Weston, *Scala for Java Developers*, https://doi.org/10.1007/978-1-4842-3108-1_14

You don't have to use `apply` methods as factory methods though. Most people end up using them to make their class APIs more succinct. This is key to how Scala can help make APIs more expressive. If it makes sense that a default behavior of your class is to create an instance, fine, but you can also make other methods look like function calls using `apply`.

So far, we've been using an `apply` method on a singleton object (`object Customer`) and dropping the `apply`, but you can have `apply` methods on a class and call them on an instance variable.

For example, we could create a class called `Adder` and call the `apply` method on an instance to add two numbers together.

```scala
// scala
class Adder {
  def apply(a: Int, b: Int) = a + b
}

val add = new Adder()
add.apply(1, 3)
```

But we can just as easily drop it and it'll look like we're calling a function even though we're actually calling a method on an instance variable.

```scala
val add = new Adder()
add(1, 3)
```

Another example is accessing array values. Suppose we have an array of Roman numerals.

```scala
val numerals = Array("I", "II", "III", "IV", "V", "VI", "VII")
```

To access the array using an index, the syntax is to use parentheses rather than square brackets.

```scala
numerals(5)              // yields "VI'
```

So, using the index in a loop, we could do something like this to print the entire array:

```scala
for (i <- 0 to numerals.length - 1)
  println(i + " = " + numerals(i))
```

What's interesting here is that there is an apply method on array that takes an Int. We could have written it like this:

```
numerals.apply(5) // yields "VI'
```

```
for (i <- 0 to numerals.length - 1)
  println(i + " = " + numerals.apply(i))
```

What looks like language syntax to access an array is actually just a regular method call. Scala fakes it.

The update Method

Assignment works in just the same way. For example, numerals(2) = "ii" actually calls a special method called update on the Array class (def update(i: Int, x: T)).

```
numerals(2) = "ii"
```

If Scala sees the assignment operator and can find an update method with appropriate arguments, it translates the assignment to a method call.

We can apply this idea to our own classes to make an API feel more like language syntax. Let's say we're in the business of telephony and part of that business is to maintain a directory of customer telephone numbers.

We can create a collection class to contain our directory, and initialize it to hold the telephone numbers of the four musketeers, like this:

```
class Directory {
  val numbers = scala.collection.mutable.Map(
    "Athos"      -> "7781 456782",
    "Aramis"     -> "7781 823422",
    "Porthos"    -> "1471 342383",
    "D`Artagnan" -> "7715 632982"
  )
}
```

If we decide that the shorthand or default behavior of the directory should be to return the telephone number of a customer, we can implement the apply method as follows:

```scala
def apply(name: String) = {
  numbers.get(name)
}
```

That way, after creating an instance of our directory, we can print Athos's number like this:

```scala
val yellowPages = new Directory()
println("Athos's telephone number : " + yellowPages("Athos"))
```

Then if we want to update a number, we could implement an updating method and call it directly. Scala's assignment shorthand means that if we actually name our method update, we can use the assignment operator and it will call the update method for us.

So, we add an update method.

```scala
def update(name: String, number: String) = {
  numbers.update(name, number)
}
```

Then we can call it to update a number like this:

```scala
yellowPages.update("Athos", "Unlisted")
```

Taking advantage of the shorthand notation, you can also use assignment.

```scala
yellowPages("Athos") = "Unlisted"
```

Multiple update Methods

We could also add a second update method, this time with an Int as the first argument.

```scala
def update(areaCode: Int, newAreaCode: String) = {
  ???
}
```

Let's say we want it to update an area code across all entries. We could enumerate each entry to work out which numbers start with the area code from the first argument. For any that match, we go back to the original map and update the entry.

```
def update(areaCode: Int, newAreaCode: String) = {
  numbers.foreach(entry => {
    if (entry._2.startsWith(areaCode.toString))
      numbers(entry._1) = entry._2.replace(areaCode.toString, newAreaCode)
  })
}
```

The _1 and _2 are Scala notation for accessing what's called a *tuple*. It's a simple data structure that we're using to treat what, in our case, would be a Map.Entry in Java as a single variable. The _1 and _2 are method calls that let us access the *key* and *value* respectively. Tuples are actually more general purpose than this and not just used for maps. We're using a tuple of two elements (a Tuple2) but you can have tuples with up to 22 elements (Tuple22).

We can call the new update method using the shorthand assignment syntax like this:

```
object DirectoryExampleAlternativeUpdateMethod extends App {
  val yellowPages = new Directory
  println(yellowPages)

  yellowPages(7781) = "7555"
  println(yellowPages)
}
```

The outcome of this is that both Athos and Aramis will have their area codes updated.

Multiple Arguments to update

You can have as many arguments in the update method as you like but only the last will be used as the updated value. This makes sense, as you can only have one value to the right of an assignment operator.

The rest of the argument list is used to select the appropriate update methods. So, if you had another method with three arguments (areaCode, anotherArgument, and newAreaCode) like this:

```
def update(areaCode: Int, another: String, newAreaCode: String) = ???
```

...the types would be used to work out which update method should be called on assignment.

```
yellowPages(7998) = "7668"
yellowPages(7998, "another argument") = "???"
```

Summary

We've seen more about the apply method in this chapter; how you don't just use it for factory-style creation methods but also for building rich APIs. You can make client code more concise by making method calls look like function calls.

We also saw how the related update method works and in the same way how we can write APIs that take advantage of the assignment operator and implement custom update behavior.

CHAPTER 15

Faking Language Constructs

Scala allows you to write your code in such a way as to give the impression that you're working with native language constructs, when really you're just working with regular methods.

This chapter will cover the following:

- How Scala allows you to use curly braces instead of regular parentheses when calling methods.

- How Scala supports higher-order functions: functions that take functions as arguments and return functions as results.

- How Scala supports currying out of the box.

These things don't sound that impressive, but combined they allow for a surprising amount of flexibility. We'll see how these techniques can help you write more flexible and readable code.

All the code samples in this chapter are in Scala.

Curly Braces (and Function Literals)

There's a simple rule in Scala.

> Any method call that accepts exactly one argument can use curly braces to surround the argument instead of parentheses.

So, instead of this:

```
numerals.foreach(println(_))
```

© Toby Weston 2018
T. Weston, *Scala for Java Developers*, https://doi.org/10.1007/978-1-4842-3108-1_15

...you can write this:

```
numerals.foreach{println(_)}
```

All we've done is swap the brackets for curly braces. Not very impressive, but things start to look a bit more interesting when we introduce some new lines.

```
numerals.foreach {
  println(_)
}
```

Now it begins to look like a built-in control structure. Developers are used to interpreting curly braces as demarcation of language syntax. So, this looks more like the built-in for loop, even though it's just a method call.

The main reason for doing this is to allow clients to pass in functions as arguments in a natural and concise way. When you write functions that can take functions as arguments, you're creating *higher-order* functions. These allow for greater flexibility and re-use.

For example, let's say we want to do some work and update a UI element, like a progress bar or a customer basket. The best way to do this is in a new thread so that we don't slow down the main UI thread and cause pauses for the user.

Higher-Order Functions

If every call to update a UI element must be done on its own thread, we might end up with a naive implementation like this:

```
object Ui {
  def updateUiElements() {
    new Thread() {
      override def run(): Unit = updateCustomerBasket(basket)
    }.start()

    new Thread() {
      override def run(): Unit = updateOffersFor(customer)
    }.start()
  }
}
```

The Ui object executes the sequence of updates one after another, each on a new thread. The Ui object is managing the threading policy *and* the update behavior. It would be better if something else was responsible for coordinating threading and the Ui object was left to the update behavior. That way, we could avoid duplication and if the threading policy changes, we wouldn't have to find all the usages scattered about the place.

The solution is to define a function that can run some other function on a thread. We could create a function called runInThread with the boilerplate threading code.

```
def runInThread() {
  new Thread() {
    override def run(): Unit = ???
  }.start()
}
```

It will create and start a new thread but it doesn't do anything interesting. How do we pass in a function? In Java, you'd probably pass in an anonymous instance of a Runnable or Callable or a lambda.

You do the same in Scala but rather than pass in a functional interface as the argument, you pass in a shorthand signature denoting a function argument. You define a variable as usual (function in the following example) but the type that follows the colon represents a function. Our example has no arguments and returns a value of Unit. It's equivalent to Java's signature for a lambda: () -> Void.

```
def runInThread(function: () => Unit) {
  new Thread() {
    override def run(): Unit = ???
  }.start()
}
```

Then we just execute the function in the body of the thread. Remember the brackets denote the shorthand for executing the apply method.

```
def runInThread(function: () => Unit) {
  new Thread() {
    override def run(): Unit = function()        // aka function.apply()
  }.start()
}
```

Given the new `runInThread` method, we can rewrite the UI code like this:

```
def updateUiElements() {
  runInThread(() => updateCustomerBasket(basket))
  runInThread(() => updateOffersFor(customer))
}
```

We've eliminated the duplication by passing in functions to `runInThread`.

Higher-Order Functions with Curly Braces

This doesn't really live up to the promise of clients being able to pass functions as arguments "in a natural and concise way". It looks a lot like Java's lambda syntax, but we can make it look more natural and more like language syntax if we use the curly braces.

If we just replace the parentheses with curly braces, it doesn't really improve things.

```
// yuk!
def updateUiElements() {
  runInThread { () =>
    updateCustomerBasket(basket)
  }

  runInThread { () =>
    updateOffersFor(customer)
  }
}
```

But we can employ another trick to get rid of the empty parentheses and arrows. We can use what's called a *call-by-name* parameter.

Call-by-Name

In Java, you can't do anything about an empty lambda argument list (e.g., `() -> Void`) but in Scala, you can drop the brackets from a function signature to indicate that the argument is call-by-name. To invoke it, you no longer need to call the `apply` method. Instead, you simply reference it.

```
def runInThread(function: => Unit) {          // call-by-name
  new Thread() {
    override def run(): Unit = function        // not function()
  }.start()
}
```

The by-name parameter expression isn't evaluated until it's actually used; not when it's defined. It behaves just like the longhand function did even though it looks like we're calling the function at the point where we pass it into our runInThread method.

```
def updateUiElements() {
  runInThread {
    updateCustomerBasket(basket)
  }

  runInThread {
    updateOffersFor(customer)
  }
}
```

This starts to make things look a lot more natural, especially if we want to do more within a running thread. For example, let's say we want to apply a discount before updating a customer's basket. The braces and indents make it very clear that this happens in the same thread as the update.

```
def updateUiElements() {
  runInThread {
    applyDiscountToBasket(basket)
    updateCustomerBasket(basket)
  }
  runInThread {
    updateOffersFor(customer)
  }
}
```

You can think of it as shorthand for creating a parameter-less lambda.

Call-By-Name != Lazy

People often think that by-name parameters are the same thing as *lazy values* but this isn't technically accurate. Yes, they aren't evaluated until they're encountered at runtime but, unlike true lazy values, they will be evaluated *every* time they're encountered.

True lazy values are evaluated the first time they're encountered and stored so the second time you ask for the value, it's just returned, not evaluated again.

So, by-name parameters are not lazy.

Currying

Using the `apply` method and curly braces allows us to create APIs that are expressive and natural to use. It allows us to create control abstractions that conform to what we already expect from the language in terms of syntax.

But remember what we said earlier about the curly braces rule.

> Any method call that accepts exactly one argument can use curly
> braces to surround the argument instead of parentheses.

We can only use curly braces with single-argument methods. What if we want to add an argument to our `runInThread` method and still use the elegant syntax? The good news is that it's entirely possible; we employ a technique called *currying*.

Let's extend our `runInThread` method to add a new argument to assign a thread group.

```
def runInThread(group: String, function: => Unit) {
  new Thread(new ThreadGroup(group), new Runnable() {
    def run(): Unit = function
  }).start()
}
```

As only single-argument lists can use braces, we have to regress the Ui object back to using parentheses.

```
// yuk!
def updateUiElements() {
  runInThread("basket", {
    applyDiscountToBasket(basket)
    updateCustomerBasket(basket)
  })
  runInThread("customer",
    updateOffersFor(customer)
  )
}
```

If we could convert our function with two arguments into a function that takes one argument we'd be able to use the curly braces again. Fortunately for us, that's exactly what currying is about. Currying is the process of turning a function of two or more arguments into a series of functions, each taking a single argument.

For a function of two arguments, currying would produce a function that takes one argument and returns another function. This returned function would also have a single argument (for what would have been the second argument of the original function). Confused? Let's work through an example.

Let's say we have a function f that takes two arguments, a and b, and returns $a + b$.

$$f(a, b) = a + b$$

To convert this into two functions, each with a single argument, first we create a function to take a and give back a new function (f').

$$f(a) \rightarrow f'$$

This new function should itself take a single argument, b.

$$f(a) \rightarrow f'(b)$$

That entire function should return the result, $a + b$.

$$f(a) \rightarrow f'(b) \rightarrow a + b$$

We're left with two functions (f and $\rightarrow f'$), each taking a single argument.

With the pseudo-mathematical notation on the same page, it's worth restating my original definition and comparing the original to the curried form of the function (see Figure 15-1).

Original $$f(a, b) = a + b$$

Curried $$f(a) \rightarrow f'(b) \rightarrow a + b$$

Figure 15-1. *Original function and steps to arrive at its curried form*

For a function of two arguments, currying would produce a function that takes one argument and returns another function. This returned function would also have a single argument (for what would have been the second argument of the original function).

To evaluate the functions of the curried form, we'd evaluate the first function (for example, passing in a value 1).

$$f(1)$$

This would return a function that captures the value, and, because what's returned is a function, we can just evaluate it, providing a value for the last argument (2).

$$f(1)(2)$$

At this point, both values are in scope and any computation can be applied giving the final result.

I've been using a bit of a gorilla notation[13] to get my point across here. Using a more mathematically correct notation, we could show the function as being curried by creating a new function taking a and mapping b to $a + b$.

$$f(a) = (b \rightarrow a + b)$$

If you're familiar with the lambda calculus,[14] you'll already know that $\lambda ab.a + b$ is shorthand for its curried form $\lambda a. (\lambda b.(a + b))$.

---

[13]A discussion of the notation used can be found at `http://bit.ly/1Q2bU6s`
[14]Some notes on the Lambda Calculus can be found at `http://bit.ly/1G4OdVo`

Closures

Interestingly, the process of capturing a value and making it available to a second function like this is called *closure*. It's where we get the term *closure* from when referring to anonymous functions or lambdas that capture values.

Scala Support for Curried Functions

A regular uncurried function to add two numbers might look like this:

```
def add(x: Int, y: Int): Int = x + y
```

Scala supports curried functions out of the box, so we don't need to do any manual conversion; all we do to turn this into its curried version is to separate out the arguments using parentheses.

```
def add(x: Int)(y: Int): Int = x + y
```

Scala has created two single-argument parameter lists for us. To evaluate the function, we'd do the following:

```
scala> add(1)(2)
res1: Int = 3
```

To see it in stages, we could just evaluate the first half like this:

```
scala> val f = add(1) _
f: Int => Int = <function1>
```

The underscore gives the REPL a hint about what we're trying to do. The result f is a function from Int to Int. The value 1 has been *captured* and is available to that function. So, we can now just execute the returned function supplying our second value.

```
scala> f(2)
res2: Int = 3
```

So, what does this mean for our `runInThread` method? Well, if we create a curried version of the function, we can get back to using our lovely curly braces.

We start by splitting the argument into two to create the curried form of the original.

```scala
def runInThread(group: String)(function: => Unit) {
  new Thread(new ThreadGroup(group), new Runnable() {
    def run(): Unit = function
  }).start()
}
```

Notice there are no other changes to make to the function. Inside `runInThread` everything is just as it was. However, we can now change the `Ui` object back to using curly braces for the second argument.

```scala
def updateUiElements() {
  runInThread("basket") {
    applyDiscountToBasket(basket)
    updateCustomerBasket(basket)
  }
  runInThread("customer",
    updateOffersFor(customer)
  )
}
```

Summary

With a few built-in features, Scala allows us to write methods that look like language constructs. We can use higher-order functions to create control abstractions: functions that abstract over complex behavior and reduce duplication yet still offer flexibility to the code that calls them.

We can use curly braces anywhere a single-argument method is used. We can use this to provide visual cues and patterns that are immediately recognizable. Using built-in currying support, we're not limited to using this only for single-argument functions; we can create even richer APIs by converting multiple-argument functions into multiple single-argument functions.

CHAPTER 16

Pattern Matching

As well as providing switch-like functionality (that's more powerful than Java's version), pattern matching offers a rich set of "patterns" that can be used to match against. In this chapter, we'll look at the anatomy of patterns and talk through some examples, including literal, constructor, and type query patterns.

Pattern matching also provides the ability to deconstruct matched objects, giving you access to parts of a data structure. We'll look at the mechanics of deconstruction: *extractors*, which are basically objects with the special method `unapply` implemented.

Switching

Let's start by looking at the pattern match expression from earlier.

```
val month = "August"
val quarter = month match {
  case "January" | "February" | "March"     => "1st quarter"
  case "April" | "May" | "June"             => "2nd quarter"
  case "July" | "August" | "September"      => "3rd quarter"
  case "October" | "November" | "December"  => "4th quarter"
  case _                                    => "unknown quarter"
}
```

There are several key differences between Java's `switch` and Scala's `match` expression.

- There is no fall-through behavior between cases in Scala. Java uses `break` to avoid a fall-through but Scala breaks between each case automatically.

- In Scala, a pattern match is an expression; it returns a value. Java switches must have side effects to be useful.

© Toby Weston 2018
T. Weston, *Scala for Java Developers*, https://doi.org/10.1007/978-1-4842-3108-1_16

- We can switch on a wider variety of things with Scala, not just primitives, enums, and strings. We can switch on objects, and things, that fit a "pattern" of our own design. In the example, we're using "or" to build a richer match condition.

Pattern matching also gives us the following:

- The ability to guard the conditions of a match; using an `if`, we can enrich a case to match not only on the pattern (the part straight after the `case`) but also on some binary condition.

- Exceptions for failed matches; when a value doesn't match anything at runtime, Scala will throw a `MatchError` exception letting us know.

- Optional compile-time checks: you can set it up so that if you forget to write a case to match all possible combinations, you'll get a compiler warning. This is done using what's called *sealed traits*.

Patterns

The anatomy of a match expression looks like this:

```
value match {
    case pattern guard => expression
    ...
    case _              => default
}
```

We have a value, then the `match` keyword, followed by a series of match cases. The value can itself be an expression, a literal or even an object.

Each case is made up of a pattern, optionally a guard condition, and the expression to evaluate on a successful match.

You might add a default, catch-all pattern at the end. The underscore is our first example of an actual pattern. It's the wildcard pattern and means "match on anything".

A pattern can be as follows:

- A wildcard match (_).

- A literal match, meaning equality, used for values such as 101 or RED.

- A constructor match, meaning that a value would match if it could have been created using a specific constructor.

- A deconstruction match, otherwise known as an *extractor* pattern.

- A match based on a specific type, known as a type query pattern.

- A pattern with alternatives (specified with |).

Patterns can also include a variable name, which on matching will be available to the expression on the right-hand side. It's what's referred to as a variable ID in the language specification.

There are some more which I've left off; if you're interested see the Pattern Matching section of the Scala Language Specification.[15]

Literal Matches

A literal match is a match against any Scala literal. The following example uses a string literal and has similar semantics to a Java switch statement.

```scala
val language = "French"
value match {
    case "french" => println("Salut")
    case "French" => println("Bonjour")
    case "German" => println("Guten Tag")
    case _        => println("Hi")
}
```

The value must exactly match the literal in the case. In the example, the result will be to print "Bonjour" and not "Salut" as the match value has a capital F. The match is based on equality (==).

---

[15]http://www.scala-lang.org/files/archive/spec/2.12/08-pattern-matching.html

Constructor Matches

Constructor patterns allow you to match a case against how an object was *constructed*. Let's say we have a SuperHero class that looks like this:

case class
  SuperHero(heroName: **String**, alterEgo: **String**, powers: **List**[**String**])

It's a regular class with three constructor arguments, but the keyword case at the beginning designates it as a *case class*. For now, that just means that Scala will automatically supply a bunch of useful methods for us, like hashCode, equals, and toString.

Given the class and its fields, we can create a match expression like this:

```
1    object BasicConstructorPatternExample extends App {
2      val hero =
3        new SuperHero("Batman", "Bruce Wayne", List("Speed", "Agility"))
4
5      hero match {
6        case SuperHero(_, "Bruce Wayne", _) => println("I'm Batman!")
7        case SuperHero(_, _, _)             => println("???")
8      }
9    }
```

Using a constructor pattern, it will match for any hero whose alterEgo field matches the value "Bruce Wayne" and print "I'm Batman!". For everyone else, it'll print question marks.

The underscores are used as placeholders for the constructor arguments; you need three on the second case (line 7) because the constructor has three arguments. The underscore means you don't care what their values are. Putting the value "Bruce Wayne" on line 6 means you do care and that the second argument to the constructor must match it.

With constructor patterns, the value must also match the type. Let's say that SuperHero is a subtype of a Person, as shown in Figure 16-1.

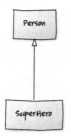

Figure 16-1. *SuperHero is a subtype of Person*

If the hero variable was actually an instance of Person and not a SuperHero, nothing would match. In the case of no match, you'd see a MatchError exception at runtime. To avoid the MatchError, you'd need to allow non-SuperHero types to match. To do that, you could just use a wildcard as a default.

```
object BasicConstructorPatternExample extends App {
  val hero = new Person("Joe Ordinary")

  hero match {
    case SuperHero(_, "Bruce Wayne", _) => println("I'm Batman!")
    case SuperHero(_, _, _)             => println("???")
    case _                              => println("I'm a civilian")
  }
}
```

Patterns can also bind a matched value to a variable. Instead of just matching against a literal (like "Bruce Wayne") we can use a variable as a placeholder and access a matched value in the expression on the right-hand side. For example, we could ask the following question:

> "What super-powers does an otherwise unknown person have, if they *are* a superhero with the alter ego Bruce Wayne?"

```
1  def superPowersFor(person: Person) = {
2    person match {
3      case SuperHero(_, "Bruce Wayne", powers) => powers
4      case _                                   => List()
5    }
6  }
7
8  println("Bruce has the following powers " + superPowersFor(person))
```

We're still matching only on types of SuperHero with a literal match against their alter ego, but this time the underscore in the last position on line 3 is replaced with the variable powers. This means we can use the variable on the right-hand side. In this case, we just return it to answer the question.

Variable binding is one of pattern matching's key strengths. In practice, it doesn't make much sense to use a literal value like "Bruce Wayne" as it limits the application. Instead, you're more likely to replace it with either a variable or wildcard pattern.

```
object HeroConstructorPatternExample extends App {
  def superPowersFor(person: Person) = {
    person match {
      case SuperHero(_, _, powers) => powers
      case _                       => List()
    }
  }
}
```

You'd then use values from the match object as input. To find out what powers Bruce Wayne has, you'd pass in a SuperHero instance for Bruce.

```
val bruce =
  new SuperHero("Batman", "Bruce Wayne", List("Speed", "Agility"))
println("Bruce has the following powers: " + superPowersFor(bruce))
```

The example is a little contrived as we're using a match expression to return something that we already know. But as we've made the superPowersFor method more general purpose, we could also find out what powers any superhero or regular person has.

```
val steve =
  new SuperHero("Capt America", "Steve Rogers", List("Tactics", "Speed"))
val jayne = new Person("Jayne Doe")

println("Steve has the following powers: " + superPowersFor(steve))
println("Jayne has the following powers: " + superPowersFor(jayne))
```

> **Constructor Patterns**
>
> Note that constructor patterns work on case classes out of the box. Technically, this is because they automatically implement a special method called unapply. We'll see shortly how you can implement your own and achieve the same kind of thing for non-case classes.

Type Query

Using a constructor pattern, you can implicitly match against a type and access its fields. If you don't care about the fields, you can use a type query to match against just the type.

For example, we could create a method nameFor to give us a person or superhero's name, and call it with a list of people. We'd get back either their name, or if they're a superhero, their alter ego.

```
1   object HeroTypePatternExample extends App {
2
3     val batman =
4       new SuperHero("Batman", "Bruce Wayne", List("Speed", "Agility"))
5     val cap =
6       new SuperHero("Capt America", "Steve Rogers", List("Tactics",
          "Speed"))
7     val jayne = new Person("Jayne Doe")
8
9     def nameFor(person: Person) = {
10      person match {
11        case hero: SuperHero => hero.alterEgo
12        case person: Person => person.name
13      }
14    }
15
16    // What's a superhero's alter ego?
17    println("Batman's Alter ego is " + nameFor(batman))
18    println("Captain America's Alter ego is " + nameFor(cap))
19    println("Jayne's Alter ego is " + nameFor(jayne))
20  }
```

Rather than use a sequence of instanceOf checks followed by a cast, you can specify a variable and type. In the expression that follows the arrow, the variable can be used as an instance of that type. So, on line 11, hero is magically an instance of SuperHero and SuperHero specific methods (like alterEgo) are available without casting.

When you use pattern matching to deal with exceptions in a try and catch, it's actually type queries that are being used.

```
try {
  val url = new URL("http://baddotrobot.com")
  val reader = new BufferedReader(new InputStreamReader(url.openStream))
  var line = reader.readLine
  while (line != null) {
    line = reader.readLine
    println(line)
  }
} catch {
  case _: MalformedURLException => println("Bad URL")
  case e: IOException => println("Problem reading data : " + e.getMessage)
}
```

The underscore in the MalformedURLException match shows that you can use a wildcard with type queries if you're not interested in using the value.

Deconstruction Matches and unapply

It's common to implement the apply method as a factory-style creation method; a method taking arguments and giving back a new instance. You can think of the special case unapply method as the opposite of this. It takes an instance and extracts values from it; usually the values that were used to construct it.

$$apply\ (a,\ b) \rightarrow object\ (a,\ b)$$

$$unapply\ (object\ (a,\ b))) \rightarrow a,\ b$$

Because they extract values, objects that implement unapply are referred to as *extractors*.

Given an object, an *extractor* typically extracts the parameters that would have created that object.

So, if we want to use our `Customer` in a match expression, we'd add an `unapply` method to its companion object. Let's start to build this up.

```scala
class Customer(val name: String, val address: String)

object Customer {
  def unapply(???) = ???
}
```

An unapply method always takes an instance of the object you'd like to deconstruct, in our case a `Customer`.

```scala
object Customer {
  def unapply(customer: Customer) = ???
}
```

It should return either the extracted parts of the object or something to indicate it couldn't be deconstructed. In Scala, rather than return a null to represent this, we return the *option* of a result. It's the same idea as the `Optional` class in Java.

```scala
object Customer {
  def unapply(customer: Customer): Option[???] = ???
}
```

The last piece of the puzzle is to work out what can optionally be extracted from the object: the type to put in the `Option` parameter. If you wanted to be able to extract just the customer name, the return would be `Option[String]`, but we want to be able to extract both the name and address (and therefore be able to match on both name and address in a match expression).

The answer is to use a tuple, the data structure we saw earlier. It's a way of returning multiple pieces of data in a single type.

```scala
object Customer {
  def unapply(customer: Customer): Option[(String, String)] = {
    Some((customer.name, customer.address))
  }
}
```

We can now use a pattern match with our customer.

```
val customer = new Customer("Bob", "1 Church street")
customer match {
  case Customer(name, address) => println(name + " " + address)
}
```

You'll notice that this looks like our constructor pattern example. That's because it's essentially the same thing; we used a case class before, which added an unapply method for us. This time we created it ourselves. It's both an *extractor* and, because there's a symmetry with the constructor, a constructor pattern.

More specifically, the list of values to extract in a pattern must match those in a class's primary constructor to be called a constructor pattern. See the language spec[16] for details.

Why Write Your Own Extractors?

Why would you implement your own extractor method (unapply) when case classes already have one? It might be simply because you can't or don't want to use a case class or you may not want the match behavior of a case class; you might want custom extraction behavior (for example, returning Boolean from unapply to indicate a match with no extraction).

It might also be the case that you can't modify a class but you'd like to be able to extract parts from it. You can write extractors for anything. For example, you can't modify the String class but you still might want to extract things from it, like parts of an email address or a URL.

For example, the stand-alone object in the following example extracts the protocol and host from a string when it's a valid URL. It has no relationship with the String class but still allows us to write a match expression and "deconstruct" a string into a protocol and host.

```
object UrlExtractor {
  def unapply(string: String): Option[(String, String)] = {
    try {
      val url = new URL(string)
```

---

[16]http://www.scala-lang.org/files/archive/spec/2.12/08-pattern-matching.html

```scala
      Some((url.getProtocol, url.getHost))
    } catch {
      case _: MalformedURLException => None
    }
  }
}


val url = "http://baddotrobot.com" match {
  case UrlExtractor(protocol, host) => println(protocol + " " + host)
}
```

This decoupling between patterns and the data types they work against is called *representation independence* (see Section 24.6 of *Programming in Scala*).[17]

Guard Conditions

You can complement the patterns we've seen with `if` conditions.

```scala
customer.yearsACustomer = 3
  val discount = customer match {
    case YearsACustomer(years) if years >= 5 => Discount(0.50)
    case YearsACustomer(years) if years >= 2 => Discount(0.20)
    case YearsACustomer(years) if years >= 1 => Discount(0.10)
    case _ if blackFriday(today)            => Discount(0.10)
    case _                                  => Discount(0)
  }
```

The condition following the pattern is called a *guard*. You can reference a variable if you like, so we can say for customers of over five years, a 50% discount applies; two years, 20%, and so on. If a variable isn't required, that's fine too. For example, we've got a case that says if no previous discount applies and today is Black Friday, give a discount of 10%.

---

[17]http://www.artima.com/pins1ed/extractors.html

CHAPTER 17

Map and FlatMap

In this chapter, we'll look at some of the functional programming features of Scala, specifically the ubiquitous map and flatMap functions. We're interested in these because they're closely related to the idea of monads, a key feature of functional programming.

Mapping Functions

You'll see the map function on countless classes in Scala. It's often described in the context of collections. Classes like List, Set, and Map all have it. For these, it applies a given function to each element in the collection, giving back a new collection based on the result of that function. You "map" some function over each element of your collection.

For example, you could create a function that works out how old a person is today, given the year of their birth.

```
import java.util.Calendar
def age(birthYear: Int) = {
  val currentYear = Calendar.getInstance.get(Calendar.YEAR)
  currentYear - birthYear
}
```

We could call the map function on a list of birth years, passing in the function to create a new list of ages.

```
val birthdays = List(1990, 1977, 1984, 1961, 1973)
birthdays.map(age)
```

The result would be a list of ages. Assuming it's run in 2017, we can transform the year 1990 into age 27, for example.

```
res0: List[Int] = List(25, 38, 31, 54, 42)
```

171

© Toby Weston 2018
T. Weston, *Scala for Java Developers*, https://doi.org/10.1007/978-1-4842-3108-1_17

Being a higher-order function, you could have written the function inline as a lambda like this:

```
birthdays.map(year => Calendar.getInstance.get(Calendar.YEAR) - year)
```

Using the underscore as a shorthand for the lambda's parameter, it would look like this:

```
birthdays.map(Calendar.getInstance.get(Calendar.YEAR) - _)
```

It's Like foreach

So, map is a transforming function. For collections, it iterates over the collection applying some function, just like foreach does. The difference is that unlike foreach, map will collect the return values from the function into a new collection and then return that collection.

It's trivial to implement a mapping function by hand. For example, we could create a class Mappable that takes a number of elements of type A and creates a map function.

```
class Mappable[A](val elements: List[A]) {
  def map[B](f: Function1[A, B]): List[B] = {
    ???
  }
}
```

The parameter to map is a function that transforms from type A to type B; it takes an A and returns a B. I've written it longhand as a type of Function1 which is equivalent to Java's java.util.function.Function class. We can also write it using Scala's shorthand syntax and the compiler will do the conversion for us.

```
def map[B](f: A => B): List[B] = ...
```

Then it's just a question of creating a new collection, calling the function (using apply) with each element as the argument. We'd store the result to the new collection and finally return it.

```
class Mappable[A](val elements: List[A]) {
  def map[B](f: A => B): List[B] = {
    val result = collection.mutable.MutableList[B]()
    elements.foreach {
```

```
      result += f.apply(_)
    }
    result.toList
  }
}
```

We can test it by creating a list of numbers, making them "mappable" by creating a new instance of Mappable and calling map with an anonymous function that simply doubles the input.

```
object Example extends App {
  val numbers: List[Int] = List(1, 2, 54, 4, 12, 43, 54, 23, 34)
  val mappable: Mappable[Int] = new Mappable(numbers)
  val result = mappable.map(_ * 2)
  println(result)
}
```

The output would look like this:

```
List(2, 4, 108, 8, 24, 86, 108, 46, 68)
```

Recursion

This is a fairly typical iterative implementation; a more Scala-esq implementation would use recursion. See the code listings in Appendix A for some examples.

FlatMap

You'll often see the flatMap function where you see the map function. For collections, it's very similar in that it maps a function over the collection, storing the result in a new collection, but with a couple of differences.

- It still transforms but this time the function applies a one-to-many transformation. It takes a single argument as before but returns multiple values.

- The result would therefore end up being a collection of collections, so flatMap also flattens the result to give a single collection.

So,

- For a given collection of A, the map function applies a function to each element transforming an A to B. The result is a collection of B (that is, List[B]).

- For a given collection of A, the flatMap function applies a function to each element transforming an A to a collection of B. This results in a collection of collection of B (that is, List[List[B]]), which is the flattened to a single collection of B (that is, List[B]).

Let's say we want a mapping function to return a person's age plus or minus a year. So, if we think a person is 38, we'd return a list of 37, 38, 39.

```
import java.util.Calendar
def ageEitherSide(birthYear: Int): List[Int] = {
  val today = Calendar.getInstance.get(Calendar.YEAR)
  List(today - 1 - birthYear, today - birthYear, today + 1 - birthYear)
}
```

The signature has changed from the previous example to return a List[Int] rather than just an Int. If we pass the list of birthday years into the map function, we get a list of lists back (res0 below).

```
val birthdays = List(1990, 1977, 1984)

birthdays.map(ageEitherSide)

scala> birthdays.map(ageEitherSide)
res0: List[List[Int]] =
  List(List(26, 27, 28), List(39, 40, 41), List(32, 33, 34))
```

If, however, we pass it into the flatMap function, we get a flattened list back. It maps, then flattens.

```
scala> birthdays.flatMap(ageEitherSide)
res1: List[Int] = List(26, 27, 28, 39, 40, 41, 32, 33, 34)
```

If you wanted to write your own version of flatMap, it might look something like this (notice the return type of the function):

```scala
class FlatMappable[A](elements: A*) {

  def flatMap[B](f: A => List[B]): List[B] = {
    val result = collection.mutable.MutableList[B]()
    elements.foreach {
      f.apply(_).foreach {
        result += _
      }
    }
    result.toList
  }
}
```

The first loop will enumerate the elements of the collection and apply the function to each. Because this function itself returns a list, another loop is needed to enumerate each of *these*, adding them into the result collection. This is the bit that flattens the function's result.

To test it, let's start by creating a function that goes from an Int to a collection of Int. It gives back all the odd numbers between zero and the argument.

```scala
def oddNumbersTo(end: Int): List[Int] = {
  val odds = collection.mutable.MutableList[Int]()
  for (i <- 0 to end) {
    if (i % 2 != 0) odds += i
  }
  odds.toList
}
```

We then just create an instance of our class with a few numbers in. Call flatMap and you'll see that all odd numbers from 0 to 1, 0 to 2, and 0 to 10 are collected into a list.

```scala
object Example {
  def main(args: Array[String]) {
    val mappable = new FlatMappable(1, 2, 10)
    val result = mappable.flatMap(oddNumbersTo)
```

```
      println(result)
    }
  }
```

The output would be the following:

```
List(1, 1, 1, 3, 5, 7, 9)
```

Not Just for Collections

We've seen how map and flatMap work for collections, but they also exist on many other classes. More generally, map and flatMap operate on what's called *monads*. In fact, having map and flatMap behavior is one of the defining features of monads.

So just what are monads? We'll look at that next.

CHAPTER 18

Monads

Monads are one of those things that people love to talk about but which remain elusive and mysterious. If you've done any reading on functional programming, you will have come across the term.

Despite all the literature, the subject is often not well understood, partly because monads come from the abstract mathematics field of *category theory* and partly because, in programming languages, Haskell dominates the literature. Neither Haskell nor category theory are particularly relevant to the mainstream developer and both bring with them concepts and terminology that can be challenging to get your head around.

The good news is that you don't have to worry about any of that stuff. You don't need to understand category theory for functional programming. You don't need to understand Haskell to program with Scala.

Basic Definition

A layman's definition of a monad might be:

> Something that has `map` and `flatMap` functions.

This isn't the full story, but it will serve us as a starting point.

We've already seen that collections in Scala are all monads. It's useful to transform these with `map` and flatten one-to-many transformations with `flatMap`. But `map` and `flatMap` do different things on different types of monads.

Option

Let's take the `Option` class. You can use `Option` as a way of avoiding nulls, but just how does it avoid nulls and what has it got to do with monads? There are two parts to the answer.

© Toby Weston 2018
T. Weston, *Scala for Java Developers*, https://doi.org/10.1007/978-1-4842-3108-1_18

1. You avoid returning null by returning a subtype of Option to represent no value (None) or a wrapper around a value (Some). As both "no value" and "some value" are of type Option, you can treat them consistently. You should never need to say "if not null".

2. How you actually go about treating Option consistently is to use the monadic methods map and flatMap. So, Option *is a monad*.

Null Object Pattern

If you've ever seen the *Null Object pattern*, you'll notice it's a similar idea. The Null Object pattern allows you to replace a type with a subtype to represent no value. You can call methods on the instance as if it were a real value but it essentially does nothing. It's substitutable for a real value but usually has no side effects.

The main difference is that the methods you can call, defined by the instance's super-type, are usually business methods. The common methods of a monad are map and flatMap and are lower-level, functional programming abstractions.

We know what map and flatMap do for collections, but what do they do for an Option?

The map Function

The map function still transforms an object, but it's an optional transformation. It will apply the mapping function to the value of an option, *if* it has a value. The value and no value options are implemented as subclasses of Option: Some and None respectively (see Figure 18-1).

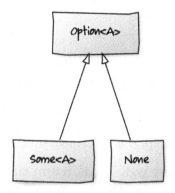

Figure 18-1. *The* Option *classes*

A mapping only applies if the option is an instance of Some. If it has no value (that is, it's an instance of None), it will simply return another None.

This is useful when you want to transform something but not worry about checking if it's null. For example, we might have a Customers trait with repository methods add and find. What should we do in implementations of find when a customer doesn't exist?

```
trait Customers extends Iterable[Customer] {
  def add(Customer: Customer)
  def find(name: String): Customer
}
```

A typical Java implementation would likely return null or throw some kind of NotFoundException. For example, the following Set-based implementation returns a null if the customer cannot be found:

```
import scala.collections._

class CustomerSet extends Customers {
  private val customers = mutable.Set[Customer]()

  def add(customer: Customer) = customers.add(customer)

  def find(name: String): Customer = {
    for (customer <- customers) {
      if (customer.name == name)
        return customer
    }
```

```
    null
  }

  def iterator: Iterator[Customer] = customers.iterator
}
```

Returning null and throwing exceptions both have similar drawbacks.

Neither communicate intent very well. If you return null, clients need to know that's a possibility so they can avoid a NullPointerException. But what's the best way to communicate that to clients? ScalaDoc? Ask them to look at the source? Both are easy for clients to miss. Exceptions may be somewhat clearer but, as Scala exceptions are unchecked, they're just as easy for clients to miss.

You also force unhappy path handling to your clients. Assuming that consumers do know to check for a null, you're asking multiple clients to implement defensive strategies for the unhappy path. You're forcing null checks on people and can't ensure consistency, or even that people will bother.

Defining the find method to return an Option improves the situation. In the following, if we find a match, we return Some customer or None otherwise. This communicates at an API level that the return type is optional. The type system forces a consistent way of dealing with the unhappy path.

```
trait Customers extends Iterable[Customer] {
  def add(Customer: Customer)
  def find(name: String): Option[Customer]
}
```

Our implementation of find can then return either a Some or a None.

```
def find(name: String): Option[Customer] = {
  for (customer <- customers) {
    if (customer.name == name)
      return Some(customer)
  }
  None
}
```

Let's say that we'd like to find a customer and get their total shopping basket value. Using a method that can return null, clients would have to do something like the following, as Albert may not be in the repository.

```
val albert = customers.find("Albert")         // can return null
val basket = if (albert != null) albert.total else 0D
```

If we use Option, we can use map to transform from an option of a Customer to an option of their basket value.

```
val basketValue: Option[Double] =
  customers.find("A").map(customer => customer.total)
```

Notice that the return type here is an Option[Double]. If Albert isn't found, map will return a None to represent no basket value. Remember that the map on Option is an optional transformation.

When you want to actually get hold of the value, you need to get it out of the Option wrapper. The API of Option will only allow you call get, getOrElse or continue processing monadically using map and flatMap.

Option.get

To get the raw value, you can use the get method but it will throw an exception if you call it against no value. Calling it is a bit of a smell as it's roughly equivalent to ignoring the possibility of a NullPointerException. You should only call it when you know the option is a Some.

```
// could throw an exception
val basketValue = customers.find("A").map(customer => customer.total).get
```

To ensure the value is a Some, you could pattern match like the following, but again, it's really just an elaborate null check.

```
val basketValue: Double = customers.find("Missing") match {
  case Some(customer) => customer.total         // avoids the exception
  case None => 0D
}
```

Option.getOrElse

Calling getOrElse is often a better choice as it forces you to provide a default value. It has the same effect as the pattern match version, but with less code.

```
val basketValue =
    customers.find("A").map(customer => customer.total).getOrElse(0D)
```

Monadically Processing Option

If you want to avoid using get or getOrElse, you can use the monadic methods on Option. To demonstrate this, we need a slightly more elaborate example. Let's say we want to sum the basket value of a subset of customers. We could create the list of names of customers we're interested in and find each of these by transforming (mapping) the customer names into a collection of Customer objects.

In the following example, we create a customer database, adding some sample data before mapping.

```
val database = new CustomerSet()

val address1 = Some(Address("1a Bridge St", None))
val address2 = Some(Address("2 Short Road", Some("AL1 2PY")))
val address3 = Some(Address("221b Baker St", Some("NW1")))

database.add(Customer("Albert", address1))
database.add(Customer("Beatriz", None))
database.add(Customer("Carol", address2))
database.add(Customer("Sherlock", address3))

val customers = Set("Albert", "Beatriz", "Carol", "Dave", "Erin")
customers.map(database.find(_))
```

We can then transform the customers again to a collection of their basket totals.

```
customers.map(database.find(_).map(_.total))
```

Now here's the interesting bit. If this transformation were against a value that could be null, and not an Option, we'd have to do a null check before carrying on. However, as it is an option, if the customer wasn't found, the map would just not do the transformation and return another "no value" Option.

When, finally, we want to sum all the basket values and get a grand total, we can use the built-in function sum.

```
customers.map(database.find(_).map(_.total)).sum          // wrong!
```

However, this isn't quite right. Chaining the two map functions gives a return type of Set[Option[Double]], and we can't sum that. We need to flatten this down to a sequence of doubles before summing.

```
customers.map(database.find(_).map(_.total)).flatten.sum
                                             ^
```

notice the position here, we map immediately on **Option**

The flattening will discard any Nones, so afterwards the collection size will be 3. Only Albert, Carol, and Beatriz's baskets get summed.

The **Option.flatMap** Function

In the preceding example, we replicated flatMap behavior by mapping and then flattening, but we could have used flatMap on Option directly.

The first step is to call flatMap on the names instead of map. As flatMap does the mapping and then flattens, we immediately get a collection of Customer.

```
val r: Set[Customer] = customers.flatMap(name => database.find(name))
```

The flatten part drops all the Nones, so the result is guaranteed to contain only customers that exist in our repository. We can then simply transform those customers to their basket total, before summing.

```
customers
  .flatMap(name => database.find(name))
  .map(customer => customer.total)
  .sum
```

Dropping the no value options is a key behavior for flatMap here. For example, compare the flatten on a list of lists as follows:

```
scala> val x = List(List(1, 2), List(3), List(4, 5))
x: List[List[Int]] = List(List(1), List(2), List(3))

scala> x.flatten
res0: List[Int] = List(1, 2, 3, 4, 5)
```

...to a list of options.

```
scala> val y = List(Some("A"), None, Some("B"))
y: List[Option[String]] = List(Some(A), None, Some(B))

scala> y.flatten
res1: List[String] = List(A, B)
```

More Formal Definition

As a more formal definition, a monad must:

- Operate on a parameterized type, which implies it's a "container" for another type (this is called a *type constructor*).

- Have a way to construct the monad from its underlying type (the *unit function*).

- Provide a flatMap operation (sometimes called *bind*).

Option and List both meet these criteria, as shown in Table 18-1.

Table 18-1. *Monad criteria met by Option and List*

	Option	**List**
Parameterized (type constructor)	`Option[A]`	`List[T]`
Construction (unit)	`Option.apply(x)` `Some(x)` `None`	`List(x, y, z)`
flatMap (bind)	`def flatMap[B](f: A => Option[B]): Option[B]`	`def flatMap[B](f: A => List[B]): List[B]`

The definition doesn't mention `map`, though, and our layman's definition for monad was the following:

> Something that has `map` and `flatMap` functions.

I wanted to introduce `flatMap` in terms of `map` because it always applies a mapping function before flattening. It's true that to be a monad you only have to provide `flatMap`, but in practice monads also supply a `map` function. This is because all monads are also *functors*; it's functors that more formally have to provide maps.

So, the technical answer is that providing `flatMap`, a parameterized type, and the unit function makes something a monad. But all monads are functors and `map` comes from functor (see Figure 18-2).

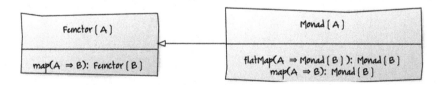

Figure 18-2. *The Functor and Monad behaviors*

Summary

In this chapter, I explained that when people talk about monadic behavior, they're really just talking about the `map` and `flatMap` functions. The semantics of `map` and `flatMap` can differ depending on the type of monad but they share a formal, albeit abstract, definition.

We looked at some concrete examples of the monadic functions on `List` and `Option`, and how we can use these with `Option` to avoid null checks. The real power of monads, though, is in "chaining" these functions to compose behavior into a sequence of simple steps. To really see this, we're going to look at some more elaborate examples in Chapter 19, and see how for comprehensions work under the covers.

CHAPTER 19

For Comprehensions

The last chapter focused on monads and the map and flatMap functions. In this chapter we're going to focus on just flatMap behavior. Specifically, we'll look at how to chain flatMap function calls before finally yielding results. For comprehensions actually use flatMap under the hood, so we'll look at the relationship in detail and explain how for comprehensions work.

Where We Left Off

Hopefully you're now comfortable with the idea of flatMap. We looked at it for the collection classes and for Option. Recall that we used flatMap to map over customer names that may or may not exist in our database. By doing so, we could sum customer basket values.

```
customers
  .flatMap(name => database.find(name))
  .map(customer => customer.total)
  .sum
```

Now let's say that we'd like to generate a shipping label for a customer. We can look up a customer in our repository and, if they have a street address and a postcode, we can generate a shipping label.

The caveats are:

1. A customer may or may not exist in the repository.

2. A given customer may or may not have an address object.

3. An address object must contain a street but may or may not contain a postcode.

© Toby Weston 2018

T. Weston, *Scala for Java Developers*, https://doi.org/10.1007/978-1-4842-3108-1_19

So, to generate a label, we need to:

1. Find a customer (who may or may not exist) by name.

2. Get the customer's address (which also may or may not exist).

3. Given the address, get the shipping information from it. (We can expect an Address object to contain a street address, but it may or may not have a postcode.)

Using Null Checks

If we were to implement this where the optionality was expressed by returning nulls, we'd be forced to do a bunch of null checks. We have four customers: Albert, Beatriz, Carol, and Sherlock. Albert has an address but no postcode, Beatriz hasn't given us her address, and the last two have full address information.

```
val customers = new CustomerSet()

val address1 = Some(Address("1a Bridge St", None))
val address2 = Some(new Address("2 Short Road", Some("AL1 2PY")))
val address3 = Some(new Address("221b Baker St", Some("NW1")))

customers.add(new Customer("Albert", address1))
customers.add(new Customer("Beatriz", None))
customers.add(new Customer("Carol", address2))
customers.add(new Customer("Sherlock", address3))
```

Given a list of customers, we can attempt to create shipping labels. As you can see, the following list includes people that don't exist in the database.

```
val all = Set("Albert", "Beatriz", "Carol", "Dave", "Erin", "Sherlock")
```

Next, we create a function to return the list of shipping labels, collecting them in a mutable set. For every name in our list, we attempt to find the customer in the database (using customers.find). As this could return null, we have to check the returned value isn't null before we can get their address.

Getting the address can return null, so we have to check for null again before getting their postcode. Once we've checked the postcode isn't null, we can finally call a method (shippingLabel) to create a label and add it to the collection. Were we to run it, only Carol and Sherlock would get through all the null checks.

```scala
import scala.collections._

val all = Set("Albert", "Beatriz", "Carol", "Dave", "Erin", "Sherlock")

def generateShippingLabels() = {
  val labels = mutable.Set[String]()
  all.foreach { name =>
    val customer: Customer = customers.find(name)
    if (customer != null) {
      val address: Address = customer.address
      if (address != null) {
        val postcode: String = address.postcode
        if (postcode != null) {
          labels.add(
              shippingLabel(customer.name, address.street, postcode))
        }
      }
    }
  }
  labels
}
  def shippingLabel(name: String, street: String, postcode: String) = {
    "Ship to:\n" + "========\n" + name + "\n" + street + "\n" + postcode
}
```

Using FlatMap with Option

If, instead of returning null for no customer, we were to use Option as the return type, we could reduce the code using flatMap.

```
1    def generateShippingLabel(): Set[String] = {
2      all.flatMap {
3        name => customers.find(name).flatMap {
4          customer => customer.address.flatMap {
5            address => address.postcode.map {
6              postcode => {
7                shippingLabel(customer.name, address.street, postcode)
8              }
9            }
10         }
11       }
12     }
13   }
14
15   def shippingLabel(name: String, street: String, postcode: String) = {
16     "Ship to:\n" + "========\n" + name + "\n" + street + "\n" + postcode
17   }
```

We start in the same way as before, by enumerating each of the names in our list, calling find on the database for each. We use flatMap to do this as we're transforming from a single customer name (String) to a monad (Option).

You can think of the option as being like a list with one element in it (either a Some or a None), so we're doing a "one-to-many"-like transformation. As we saw in the flatMap section of Chapter 17, this implies we'll need to flatten the "many" back down into "one" later, hence the flatMap.

After the initial flatMap where we find a customer in the database, we flatMap the result. If no customer was found, it wouldn't continue any further. So, on line 4, we can be sure a customer actually exists and can go ahead and get their address. As address is optional, we can flatMap again, dropping out if a customer doesn't have an address.

On line 5, we can request a customer's postcode. Postcode is optional, so only if we have one do we transform it (and the address details) into a shipping label. The map call takes care of that for us; remember that map here only applies the function (shippingLabel) when we have a value (that is, postcode is an instance of Some).

Notice that we didn't need to create a mutable collection to store the shipping label. Any transformation function like map or flatMap will produce a new collection with the transformed results. So, the final call to map on line 7 will put the shipping label into a newly created collection for us. One final comment: the resulting collection is of type String because the generateShippingLabel method returns a String.

How For Comprehensions Work

When you do a regular for loop, the compiler converts (or de-sugars) it into a method call to foreach.

```
for (i <- 0 to 5) {
  println(i)
}

// is de-sugared as

(0 to 5).foreach(println)
```

A nested loop is de-sugared like this:

```
for (i <- 0 to 5; j <- 0 to 5) {
  println(i + " " + j)
}

// is de-sugared as

(0 to 5).foreach { i =>
  (0 to 5).foreach { j =>
    println(i + " " + j)
  }
}
```

If you do a for with a yield (a for comprehension) the compiler does something different.

```
for (i <- 0 to 5) yield {
  i + 2
}
```

The yield is about returning a value. A for without a yield, although an expression, will return Unit. This is because the foreach method returns Unit. A for with a yield will return whatever is in the yield block. It's converted into a call to map rather than foreach. So, the de-sugared form of the preceding code would look like this:

```
// de-sugared form of "for (i <- 0 to 5) yield i + 2"
(0 to 5).map(i => i + 2)
```

It's mapping a sequence of numbers (0 to 5) into another sequence of numbers (2 to 7).

It's important to realize that whatever is in the yield block represents the function that's passed into map. The map itself operates on whatever is in the for part (that is, for (i <- 0 to 5)). It may be easier to recognize when we reformat the example like this:

```
for {
  i <- 0 to 5            // map operates on this collection
} yield {
  i + 2                  // the function to pass into map
}
```

It gets more interesting when we have nesting between the parentheses and the yield.

```
val x: Seq[(Int, Int)] = for {
  i <- 0 to 5
  j <- 0 to 5
} yield {
  (i, j)
}
```

Curly Braces or Parentheses?

Notice how I've used curly braces instead of parentheses in some examples? It's a more common style to use curly braces for nested for loops or loops with a yield block.

This will perform the nested loop like before but rather than translate to nested `foreach` calls, it translates to `flatMap` calls followed by a map. Again, the final map is used to transform the result using whatever is in the `yield` block.

```
// de-sugared
val x: Seq[(Int, Int)] = (0 to 5).flatMap {
  i => (0 to 5).map {
    j => (i, j)
  }
}
```

It's exactly the same as before; the `yield` block has provided the function to apply to the mapping function and what it maps over is determined by the `for` expression. In this example, we're mapping two lists of 0 to 5 to a collection of tuples, representing their Cartesian product.

```
Seq((0,0), (0,1), (0,2), (0,3), (0,4), (0,5),
    (1,0), (1,1), (1,2), (1,3), (1,4), (1,5),
    (2,0), (2,1), (2,2), (2,3), (2,4), (2,5),
    (3,0), (3,1), (3,2), (3,3), (3,4), (3,5),
    (4,0), (4,1), (4,2), (4,3), (4,4), (4,5),
    (5,0), (5,1), (5,2), (5,3), (5,4), (5,5))
```

If we break this down and go through the steps, we can see how we arrived at the de-sugared form. We start with two sequences of numbers; a and b.

```
val a = (0 to 5)
val b = (0 to 5)
```

When we map the collections, we get a collection of collections. The final `map` returns a tuple, so the return type is a sequence of sequences of tuples.

```
val x: Seq[Seq[(Int, Int)]] = a.map(i => b.map(j => (i, j)))
```

To flatten these to a collection of tuples, we have to flatten the two collections, which is what flatMap does. So, although we could do the following, it's much more straightforward to call flatMap directly.

```
val x: Seq[(Int, Int)] = a.map(i => b.map(j => (i, j))).flatten

// is equivalent to

val x: Seq[(Int, Int)] = a.flatMap(i => b.map(j => (i, j)))
```

Finally, Using a For Comprehension for Shipping Labels

What does all that mean for our shipping label example? We can convert our chained flatMap calls to use a for comprehension and neaten the whole thing up. We started with a sequence of chained calls to flatMap.

```
def generateShippingLabel_FlatMapClosingOverVariables(): Set[String] = {
  all.flatMap {
    name => customers.find(name).flatMap {
      customer => customer.address.flatMap {
        address => address.postcode.map {
          postcode => shippingLabel(name, address.street, postcode)
        }
      }
    }
  }
}
```

After converting to the for comprehension, each call to flatMap is placed in the for as a nested expression. The final one represents the map call. Its argument (the mapping function) is what's in the yield block.

```
def generateShippingLabel_ForComprehension(): Set[String] = {
  for {
    name      <- all                       // <- flatMap
    customer <- customers.find(name)       // <- flatMap
    address  <- customer.address           // <- flatMap
```

```
    postcode <- address.postcode                // <- map
  } yield {
    shippingLabel(name, address.street, postcode) // <- map argument
  }
}
```

This is much more succinct. It's easier to reason about the conditional semantics when it's presented like this; if there's no `customer` found, it won't continue to the next line. If you want to extend the nesting, you can just add another line and not be bogged down by noise or indentation.

The syntax is declarative but mimics an imperative style. It doesn't force a particular implementation on you. That's to say, with imperative `for` loops, you don't have a choice about how the loop is executed. If you wanted to do it in parallel, for example, you'd have to implement the concurrency yourself.

Using a declarative approach like this means that the underlying objects are responsible for how they execute, which gives you more flexibility. Remember, this just calls `flatMap` and classes are free to implement `flatMap` however they like.

For comprehensions work with any monad and you can use your own classes if you implement the monadic methods.

Summary

In this chapter we looked at chaining calls to `flatMap` in the context of printing shipping labels. We looked at how for comprehensions work and how they're syntactic sugar over regular Scala method calls. Specifically, we looked at loops and nested loops, how they're equivalent to calling `foreach`, how `for` loops with a `yield` block translate to mapping functions, and how nested loops with `yield` blocks translate to `flatMap` then `map` functions.

This last point is what allowed us to convert our lengthy shipping label example into a succinct `for` comprehension.

PART IV

Adopting Scala in Java Teams

You might be wondering how to adopt Scala into your existing team. The good news is that you don't need to wait for that greenfield project to start. With a bit of planning, you can integrate Scala into your existing Java projects.

In this part of the book, I'll report on some of my experiences moving existing Java projects to Scala. We'll talk about what you can expect if you try to do so. I'll outline a typical learning curve and give you one or two things to look out for, some concrete things you should be doing, and what you should be avoiding.

CHAPTER 20

Adopting Scala

Avoid Not Enough

I'd been working with Java for more than ten years before I starting looking at Scala properly. My first experience was a toe in the water. The team was naturally skeptical, so we decided to section off a part of the existing codebase to try Scala. We converted our tests to Scala and left mainline development in Java.

In hindsight, this was a terrible idea. By working only with test code, there wasn't enough critical mass or momentum to improve. The kinds of problems we were solving in test code were pretty well understood and the existing testing frameworks (like JUnit) solved most of them for us.

There didn't seem to be much scope to really use the language features. We pretty much just rewrote the tests in another testing framework, which happened to be in Scala. We didn't learn much at all and, in the end, reverted everything back to Java. It was a total waste of time and effort.

The one thing I learnt from this was that to explore a new language, you need real problems to solve: design problems, domain problems, business problems. Sectioning off a subset of your codebase limits the kinds of problems you can explore and so limits your learning.

Don't Do Too Much

The next time I had a chance to try out Scala, I went to the opposite extreme. I jumped in at the deep end, worked exclusively with Scala, and tried really hard to adopt functional programming, new patterns, new architectural designs... anything I could find that was related to Scala.

© Toby Weston 2018
T. Weston, *Scala for Java Developers*, https://doi.org/10.1007/978-1-4842-3108-1_20

I hadn't done much functional programming before, so pretty quickly I hit a wall. I was faced with concepts and ideas that were completely foreign to me. I struggled, as I was trying to learn too much, too soon: new frameworks, libraries, and techniques, as well as a new language. I tried to run before I could walk.

It took a while for me to realize that, despite being an experienced developer, I was actually a novice when it came to Scala and functional programming. I'd failed to recognize this and, in hindsight, it was irresponsible to commit to building software like this. I was hired for my expertise but managed to put barriers up, preventing me from applying that expertise.

Purely Functional FTW?

Later on, I was fortunate enough to work with some really experienced developers, all well-versed in functional programming and mostly coming from a Haskell background. This was great as I had the chance to benefit from others' experiences, and the learning curve got a little easier. After a while, the team started to adopt really advanced ideas and it soon became apparent that there was another wall to get past. We started to talk about much deeper application concerns and whether we could solve these functionally.

My point here is that, for teams not used to it, heavyweight functional programming ideas can be pretty exotic. Even in industry, I think it's fair to say that there are very few teams fully embracing this style.

I don't feel like, collectively, we can say if this extreme is helping to solve real-world business problems or not. It's just another way of doing things. It does represent a very different approach to building software from the mainstream, and for us it was perhaps a little too much. It caused a bit of a divide in the team where some people were comfortable experimenting with this approach and others weren't.

CHAPTER 21

What to Expect

The Learning Curve

If you've just started to learn Scala and are wondering what to expect, it's typical to experience a quick ramp-up in skill followed by a slower adoption of the more sophisticated features. In this chapter, I talk about what I think of as a typical learning curve.

Based on my experiences and talking to various Scala teams, we can chart a typical Scala learning curve as shown in Figure 21-1, with experience (or time) on the x axis and some measure of "learning" on the y.

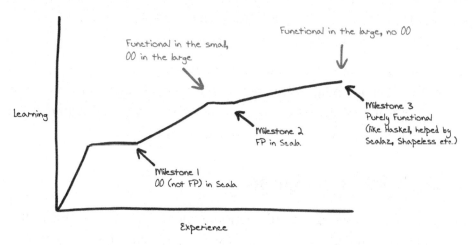

Figure 21-1. Typical Scala adoption as a learning curve

© Toby Weston 2018

T. Weston, *Scala for Java Developers*, https://doi.org/10.1007/978-1-4842-3108-1_21

Milestone 1: OO in Scala

When you first start, you can expect getting up to speed with the language to be a fairly steep incline.

"Steep" but also "short". It's not difficult to get to the first plateau, so you can expect a relatively quick increment in learning.

You'll probably sit here for a bit applying what you've learnt. I see this as the first milestone: to be able to build object-oriented or imperative applications using language-specific constructs and features, but without necessarily adopting functional programming. It's just like learning any other language in the Java/C family.

Milestone 2: FP in the Small, OO in the Large

The next milestone involves adopting functional programming techniques.

This is a much more challenging step, and likely to be a shallower curve. Typically, this will involve using traditional architecture design but implementing functional programming techniques in the small. You can think of this approach as "functional in the small, OO in the large." Starting to embrace a new functional way of thinking and unlearning some of the traditional techniques can be hard, hence the shallower incline.

Concrete examples here are more than just language syntax: things like higher-order and pure functions, referential transparency, immutability, and side effect–free, more declarative coding; all the things that are typically offered by pure functional languages. The key thing here is that they're applied in small, isolated areas.

Milestone 3: FP in the Large

The next challenge is working towards a more cohesive functional design; this really means adopting a functional style at a system level; architecting the entire application as functions and abandoning object-oriented style completely. So, aiming for something like a Haskell application.

All the concrete functional programming mechanisms mentioned here apply, but this time throughout the system; not to isolated areas but lifted to application-wide concerns. Picking up advanced libraries like Scalaz goes hand-in-hand with this part of the curve.

The Learning Continuum

You can also think of adoption of Scala as more of a continuum, with traditional imperative programming on the left and pure functional programming on the right (see Figure 21-2).

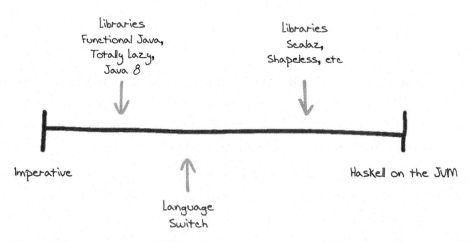

Figure 21-2. *Imperative (Java) to pure functional programming (Haskell) continuum*

You can think of the far right as Haskell on the JVM. Haskell is a pure functional language so you don't have any choice but to design your app in a functional way. Scala is an object-oriented/functional hybrid; it can only give you the tools. It can't enforce functional programming; you need discipline and experience in Scala to avoid, for example, mutating state, whereas Haskell will actually stop you.

As you start out on the continuum using Java and move to the right, libraries like Functional Java,[18] Totally Lazy,[19] and even Java 8 features[20] will help you adopt a more functional style. There comes a point where a language switch helps even more. Functional idioms become a *language feature* rather than a *library feature*. The syntactical sugar of for comphrensions are a good example.

As you carry on, using libraries like Scalaz[21] makes it easier to progress towards pure functional programming, but remember that reaching the far right, or the top-right

---

[18]http://www.functionaljava.org/

[19]https://code.google.com/p/totallylazy/

[20]https://leanpub.com/whatsnewjava8

[21]http://eed3si9n.com/learning-scalaz/index.html

quadrant of the learning curve, isn't the goal in and of itself. There are plenty of teams operating effectively across the continuum.

When you're adopting Scala, make a deliberate decision about where you want to be on the continuum, be clear about why, and use my learning curve as a way to gauge your progress.

Goals

Reaching the purely functional milestone is going to be difficult. It may not even be the right thing to do for your team. A purely functional system isn't necessarily better; I suggest that most Java teams trying to adopt Scala should aim for somewhere between Milestones 1 and 2, somewhere towards the middle of the continuum.

I think this is a good balance between seeing the benefits of the language and taking on too much. If you're working in a commercial environment, you still have to deliver software. Remember that you're potentially trading your experienced developers for novices as you move to the right. It may be better to balance your delivery commitments with your learning, since delivery risk goes up as you go to the right.

CHAPTER 22

Tips

Reflecting on my experiences I have three major tips.

1. Be clear about what you want from Scala.

2. Get guidance and share experiences.

3. Be deliberate and have a plan.

Be Clear

- **Be clear what you want out of it.** You should be asking what's in it for you. If you're going to use Scala, you should be able to explain why. Do you think being more concise will help you? Is it the benefits of functional programming? Immutability? How are you going to measure it? Will the whole team aim for a pure functional programming style like Haskell? Or OO? Decide which up front. Agree.

- **Understand the team dynamic.** Understand your team and what their wants and needs are. Gauge the team's appetite and goals. Ultimately, everyone needs to buy into the idea and head in the same direction. If one or two people feel left out or pull in another direction, you'll have problems further down the line.

- **Set expectations.** Talk to the team and management. Explain the risks and share your motivations and expectations. To set *your* expectations: learning full-on functional programming (think Haskell) is hard. Be prepared.

© Toby Weston 2018
T. Weston, *Scala for Java Developers*, https://doi.org/10.1007/978-1-4842-3108-1_22

- **Review.** Once you've started, keep reviewing where you are. Are you getting out of it what you thought you would? Can you prove or disprove any of the assumptions you started with? Is the business benefiting? If you can be more quantitative and use measurements, you can be more objective. And don't be afraid to change your mind. Maybe you discover that it's not the right choice for the team. You can always back out.

Get Guidance

- **Hire an expert.** This is my single biggest tip. If you have a real expert on the team, they can guide you through the syntax and features, and, more importantly, the adoption process. They can hold you back when you shouldn't be racing and open the door to new techniques when you're ready. It can be hard to find genuine experts but they can be worth their weight in gold.

- **Be active in the community.** Attend events, conferences, and meetups. Create a community. Learn from others and share your own experiences.

- **Look at open source.** But not too much. It's good to see how others have done things—I've certainly been exposed to some of the more exotic syntax via open source—but bear in mind that what's right for them may not be right for you. Take it with a pinch of salt. Use other people's code to inspire learning but don't copy it.

Have a Plan

- **Make a plan.** Don't just start your next project in Scala; be deliberate and have a plan.

- **Think about your goals.** Write them down, then sketch out the steps that will take you closer to you them. For example, if a goal is to get up to speed fast, you may want to run some lunchtime knowledge-sharing sessions with your team.

- **Decide where on the functional programming continuum you want to be.** Do you want to jump in at the deep end or adopt functional idioms later? One tip to minimize the learning curve is to avoid using native Scala libraries to start with. They often lead you into functional style and, at the end of the day, it's another API to learn. You can always stick with the Java libraries you know, at least to start with.

- **Make a commitment.** Commit to your goals; don't do what I did and sideline Scala to the tests. Actively decide on Scala and make a personal commitment to see it happen.

If you follow these tips, you should be clear about your goals and expectations, have an idea of where you'll get guidance from, and have planned out your next steps. You'll be facing the prospect of working with a Scala codebase, probably converting Java code and working with new tools and libraries.

In the next chapters we'll look at some practical tips on how to proceed, including converting Java code and managing your codebase.

CHAPTER 23

Convert Your Codebase

At this point, you're likely to have an existing Java codebase and may be wondering if you should try and convert the Java to Scala.

It may be a lot of effort, but I say it's definitely worth investing in converting the entire codebase to Scala if you're serious about adopting Scala. Don't aim to leave half and half. Accept that it's going to take some time and effort but commit to achieving it. If you don't finish the job, apathy can set in, not to mention that inter-op between old Java and Scala can get really awkward. You'll make your life easier if you see the job through.

IntelliJ IDEA has a convert function, which is a great starting place. It'll let you quickly turn a Java class into Scala, but be prepared: it's not often idiomatic and may not even compile without coercion. Treat any automated conversion as a learning exercise. Don't accept the transformation at face value, but look at the results and apply your judgement to tidy up. For example, rather than create a case class, IntelliJ often creates fields within the Scala class. You'll usually be able to rephrase a verbatim conversion in a more Scala-savvy way.

Consider your build tools. These will need to be updated. SBT and Maven both support mixed Java/Scala projects so there's no excuse not to keep running your continuous integration and test environments. You might also want to consider whether it's worth porting over your existing build to SBT.

© Toby Weston 2018

T. Weston, *Scala for Java Developers*, https://doi.org/10.1007/978-1-4842-3108-1_23

CHAPTER 24

Manage Your Codebase

Once you have your newly converted Scala codebase, you'll be working with it for a while. Here are some practicalities you should be aware of and some general tips to help manage your codebase.

Conventions

- There are so many syntax variations and conventions that the sheer number of syntax options available can be intimidating. **Settle on your own conventions.**

- Find a way of doing things that works for your team and stick to it. Avoid context switching between syntax modes to start with. That might mean using pattern matching rather than using map to start with. Wait until everyone is comfortable before switching over.

- Review these choices regularly as you don't want to be held back once you're up and running.

- Have a look at Twitter's efforts[22] as an example. They've managed to condense their experiences into a really practical guide. Well worth a read.

- Typesafe have a style guide,[23] which is worth reading over but should be taken with a pinch of salt.

---

[22]http://twitter.github.io/effectivescala/
[23]http://docs.scala-lang.org/style/

© Toby Weston 2018
T. Weston, *Scala for Java Developers*, https://doi.org/10.1007/978-1-4842-3108-1_24

What to Avoid

It's also great to know what to avoid when you're first starting out. I wish I knew some of these things before I started.

- **SBT can make your life harder.** SBT starts off very simple but, if you want to do anything sophisticated, it gets fairly taxing. Be prepared to do some learning; SBT isn't something that you can get very far with by cutting and pasting examples from the internet. You do actually need some understanding. I think you'll have bigger things to worry about so my suggestion is to stick with a build tool that you're familiar with to start with. It's very easy to support Scala projects in Maven.

- **Scalaz is not the place to start.** This is the Haskell programmer's library for Scala. It's hardcore and if you've not been doing purely functional programming for years, just plain avoid it. You don't need to know what an applicative functor is or why you'd use a Kleisli. At least, not to start with.

- **"Fancy" Scala libraries might not help.** When Scala first came out, a bunch of open source libraries hit the web. People got carried away and in hindsight would probably admit they went a little overboard with the syntax. As a result, there are lots of APIs that were not designed very well.

  - **Dispatch** HTTP library is a good example. The method to add a query parameter to a request is `<<?`. That just doesn't read as intuitively as `addRequestParameter`. In fairness, Dispatch offers both variants but the upshot is to be skeptical of libraries that overuse operator overloading.

  - **Anorm** is another one that offers a parser API to extract SQL results. It basically parses `ResultSets` but it has such an unintuitive DSL for doing so it makes you wonder what was wrong with doing it manually.

- **Java libraries work just fine.** You can always use the Java libraries you know and love from Scala.

- **Lack of consistency is dangerous.** We've already touched on this: don't try and use all the syntax variations at once. Figure out one properly before moving on. Keep things consistent.

Other Challenges

You'll face plenty of other challenges.

- Compilation speed is slow. It may or may not be something that concerns you but be aware: it's unlikely to match Java's speed anytime soon. In part, this is due to just how sophisticated the Scala compiler is; it does a lot of work and that comes at a price.

- Keeping your IDE build configuration in sync with your external build tool can be a challenge. Maven is so mature now that its IDE plugins pretty much handle everything for you, but the SBT plugin for IDEA on the other hand has some problems. There are third-party tools that generate IDE project files but your mileage may vary. The best I can offer is to pick the tools that seem to have the most weight behind them for your IDE.

- We've already talked about the functional programming continuum but it's worth mentioning again that it's a good idea to be mindful of where you want to be. I recommend aiming for "Functional in the small, OO in the large" to start. You'll need to continually monitor your progress and embrace the next learning challenge when you feel ready. Push the boundaries and keep learning.

APPENDIX A

Code Listings

For the full source, see https://github.com/tobyweston/learn-scala-java-devs. The following is a selection of examples from the text, expanded to provide fuller context for your reference.

Inheritance

Subtype Inheritance in Java

```java
package s4j.java.chapter12;

public class Customer implements Comparable<Customer> {

    private final String name;
    private final String address;
    private final ShoppingBasket basket = new ShoppingBasket();

    public Customer(String name, String address) {
        this.name = name;
        this.address = address;
    }

    public void add(Item item) {
        basket.add(item);
    }

    public Double total() {
        return basket.value();
    }
}
```

© Toby Weston 2018
T. Weston, *Scala for Java Developers*, https://doi.org/10.1007/978-1-4842-3108-1

```java
package s4j.java.chapter12;

public class DiscountedCustomer extends Customer {

    public DiscountedCustomer(String name, String address) {
        super(name, address);
    }

    @Override
    public Double total() {
        return super.total() * 0.90;
    }

    public Double getDiscountAmount() {
        return 10.0;
    }
}

    package s4j.java.chapter12;

    public interface Item {
        Double price();
    }

package s4j.java.chapter12;

import java.util.HashSet;
import java.util.Set;

public class ShoppingBasket {

    private final Set<Item> basket = new HashSet<>();

    public void add(Item item) {
        basket.add(item);
    }

    public Double value() {
        return basket.stream().mapToDouble(Item::price).sum();
    }
}
```

Anonymous Classes in Java

```java
package s4j.java.chapter12;

class AnonymousClass {

    public static void main(String... args) {
        Customer joe = new DiscountedCustomer("Joe", "128 Bullpen Street");

        // example of anonymous class
        joe.add(new Item() {
            @Override
            public Double price() {
                return 2.5;
            }
        });
        joe.add(new Item() {
            @Override
            public Double price() {
                return 3.5;
            }
        });

        // which can be replaced with lambdas
        joe.add(() -> 2.5);
        joe.add(() -> 3.5);

        System.out.println("Joe's basket will cost $ " + joe.total());
    }
}
```

Subtype Inheritance in Scala

```scala
package s4j.scala.chapter12

class Customer(val name: String, val address: String) extends
Ordered[Customer] {

  private final val basket: ShoppingBasket = new ShoppingBasket

  def add(item: Item) {
    basket.add(item)
  }

  def total: Double = {
    basket.value
  }
}

package s4j.scala.chapter12

class DiscountedCustomer(name: String, address: String) extends
Customer(name, address) {

  override def total: Double = {
    super.total * 0.9
  }
}

package s4j.scala.chapter12

trait Item {
  def price: Double
}

package s4j.scala.chapter12

import scala.collection.mutable

class ShoppingBasket {
  private val basket = mutable.HashSet[Item]()
```

```scala
  def add(items: Item*) {
    for (item <- items)
      basket.add(item)
  }

  def value: Double = {
    basket.map(_.price).sum
  }
}
```

Anonymous Classes in Scala

```scala
package s4j.scala.chapter12 object AnonymousClass extends App {
  val joe = new DiscountedCustomer("Joe", "128 Bullpen Street")

  // example of anonymous class
  joe.add(new Item {
    def price = 2.5
  })
  joe.add(new Item {
    def price = 3.5
  })
  println("Joe's basket will cost $ " + joe.total)
}
```

Generics

Lower Bounds in Java

Example 1

```java
package s4j.java.chapter14;

import java.util.ArrayList;
import java.util.Collections;
import java.util.List;
```

```java
/**
 * Create a basic Lion enclosure and sort the Lions within by their age.
 */
public class LowerBounds1 {

    public static <A extends Comparable<A>> void sort(List<A> list) {
        Collections.sort(list);
    }

    public static void main(String... args) {
        List<Lion> enclosure = new ArrayList<>();
        enclosure.add(new Lion());
        enclosure.add(new Lion());
        sort(enclosure);
    }

    static class Animal { }

    static class Lion extends Animal implements Comparable<Lion> {
        private Integer age;

        @Override
        public int compareTo(Lion other) {
            return this.age.compareTo(other.age);
        }
    }

    static class Zebra extends Animal { }
}
```

Example 2

```java
package s4j.java.chapter14;

import java.util.ArrayList;
import java.util.Collections;
import java.util.List;
```

```java
/**
 * Extends @{@link LowerBounds1} to create a Zoo (an enclosure with
 * different types of animal, both Lions and Zebras)
 */
public class LowerBounds2 {

    public static <A extends Comparable<A>> void sort(List<A> list) {
        Collections.sort(list);
    }

    public static void main(String... args) {
        List<Lion> enclosure = new ArrayList<>();
        enclosure.add(new Lion());
        enclosure.add(new Lion());
        sort(enclosure);                    // compiler error

        List<Animal> zoo = new ArrayList<>();
        zoo.add(new Lion());
        zoo.add(new Lion());
        zoo.add(new Zebra());
        sort(zoo);                          // won't compile if the Animal
                                            // doesn't implement Comparable
    }

    static class Animal implements Comparable<Animal> {
        @Override
        public int compareTo(Animal o) {
            return 0;
        }
    }

    static class Lion extends Animal { }
    static class Zebra extends Animal { }
}
```

Example 3

```
package s4j.java.chapter14;

import java.util.ArrayList;
import java.util.Collections;
import java.util.List;

/**
 * Extends @{@link LowerBounds2} to add ? super A in the comparator and
 * so allow sorting of the Lion enclosure
 */
public class LowerBounds3 {
    public static <A extends Comparable<? super A>> void sort(List<A> list)
{
        Collections.sort(list);
    }

    public static void main(String... args) {
        List<Lion> enclosure = new ArrayList<>();
        enclosure.add(new Lion());
        enclosure.add(new Lion());
        sort(enclosure);                // no longer a compiler failure

        List<Animal> zoo = new ArrayList<>();
        zoo.add(new Lion());
        zoo.add(new Lion());
        zoo.add(new Zebra());
        sort(zoo);
    }

    static class Animal implements Comparable<Animal> {
        @Override
        public int compareTo(Animal o) {
            return 0;
        }
    }

    static class Lion extends Animal { }
    static class Zebra extends Animal { }
}
```

Multiple Bounds in Java

Java Example 1

```java
package s4j.java.chapter14;

import java.util.ArrayList;
import java.util.Collections;
import java.util.List;

public class MultipleBounds {

    // sets two upper bounds to the generic type A
    public static <A extends Animal & Comparable<Animal>>
            void sort(List<A> list) {
        Collections.sort(list);
    }

    public static void main(String... args) {
        List<Lion> enclosure = new ArrayList<>();
        enclosure.add(new Lion());
        enclosure.add(new Lion());
        sort(enclosure);

        List<Animal> zoo = new ArrayList<>();
        zoo.add(new Lion());
        zoo.add(new Lion());
        zoo.add(new Zebra());
        sort(zoo);
    }

    static class Animal implements Comparable<Animal> {
        @Override
        public int compareTo(Animal o) {
            return 0;
        }
    }
}
```

```
    static class Lion extends Animal { }
    static class Zebra extends Animal { }
}
```

Lower Bounds in Scala

Example 1

```
package s4j.scala.chapter14

object LowerBounds1 {

  def sort[A <: Comparable[A]](list: List[A]): Unit = { ??? }

  def main(args: String*) {
    var enclosure = List[Lion]()
    enclosure = new Lion +: enclosure
    enclosure = new Lion +: enclosure
    sort(enclosure)
  }

  class Animal
  class Lion extends Animal with Comparable[Lion] {
    def compareTo(o: Lion): Int = 0
  }
  class Zebra extends Animal
}
```

Example 2

```
package s4j.scala.chapter14

object LowerBounds2 {

  def sort[A <: Comparable[A]](list: List[A]): Unit = { ??? }

  def main(args: String*) {

    var enclosure = List[Lion]()
    enclosure = new Lion +: enclosure
```

```
    enclosure = new Lion +: enclosure
    sort(enclosure)              // compiler failure

    var zoo = List[Animal]()
    zoo = new Zebra +: zoo
    zoo = new Lion +: zoo
    zoo = new Lion +: zoo
    sort(zoo)                         // wont compile if Animal
                                      // doesn't implement Comparable

  }

  class Animal extends Comparable[Animal] {
    def compareTo(o: Animal): Int = 0
  }
  class Lion extends Animal
  class Zebra extends Animal
}
```

Example 3

```
package s4j.scala.chapter14

object LowerBounds3 {

  // although a literal translation of the java, this would cause an
  // "illegal cyclic reference involving type A" error:

  // def sort[A <: Comparable[_ >: A]](a: List[A]) = { ??? }

  // instead, we use this (and provide a type hint in the sort method
  below)
  def sort[A <: Comparable[U], U >: A](list: List[A]) = { }

  def main(args: String*) {

    var enclosure = List[Lion]()
    enclosure = new Lion +: enclosure
    enclosure = new Lion +: enclosure
    sort[Lion, Animal](enclosure) // no longer a compiler failure
```

```scala
  var zoo = List[Animal]()
  zoo = new Zebra +: zoo
  zoo = new Lion +: zoo
  zoo = new Lion +: zoo
  sort(zoo)
}

class Animal extends Comparable[Animal] {
  def compareTo(o: Animal): Int = 0
}
class Lion extends Animal
class Zebra extends Animal
}
```

Multiple Bounds in Scala

Example 1

```scala
package s4j.scala.chapter14

class MultipleBounds {

  // we can't set two upper bounds like we can in Java but we can say the
  // bound type must also extend certain traits
  def sort[A <: Lion with Comparable[Animal]](list: List[A]) = { }

  def main(args: String*) {

    var enclosure = List[Lion]()
    enclosure = new Lion +: enclosure
    enclosure = new Lion +: enclosure
    // sort[Lion, Animal](enclosure)          // compiler error
    sort(enclosure)                           // must remove the type hints
  }

  class Animal extends Comparable[Animal] {
    def compareTo(o: Animal): Int = 0
  }
```

```scala
  class Lion extends Animal
  class Zebra extends Animal
}
```

Pattern Matching

Constructor Matches

Example 1

```scala
package s4j.scala.chapter18

object BasicConstructorPatternExample1 extends App {
  val hero = new SuperHero("Batman", "Bruce Wayne", List("Speed",
  "Agility"))

  hero match {
    case SuperHero(_, "Bruce Wayne", _) => println("I'm Batman!")
    case SuperHero(_, _, _)             => println("???")
  }
}
```

Example 2

```scala
package s4j.scala.chapter18

object BasicConstructorPatternExample2 extends App {
  // Joe is a Person, not a SuperHero
  val hero = new Person("Joe Ordinary")

  // produces a 'MatchError' as a Person doesn't match anything
  hero match {
    case SuperHero(_, "Bruce Wayne", _) => println("I'm Batman!")
    case SuperHero(_, _, _)             => println("???")
  }
}
```

Example 3

package s4j.scala.chapter18

```scala
object BasicConstructorPatternExample3 extends App {
  val hero = new Person("Joe Ordinary")

  // adding the wildcard _ means Joe matches the last case
  hero match {
    case SuperHero(_, "Bruce Wayne", _) => println("I'm Batman!")
    case SuperHero(_, _, _)             => println("???")
    case _                              => println("I'm a civilian")
  }
}
```

Example 4

package s4j.scala.chapter18

```scala
object HeroConstructorPatternExample extends App {
  val bruce = new SuperHero("Batman", "Bruce Wayne", List("Speed", "Agility"))
  val steve = new SuperHero("Captain America", "Steve Rogers",
List("Tactics", "Speed"))
  val jane = new Person("Jane Doe")

  def superPowersFor(person: Person) = {
    person match {
      case SuperHero(_, _, powers) => powers
      case _ => List()
    }
  }

  // What super-powers does an otherwise unknown person have, if they are a
  // superhero with the alter-ego Bruce Wayne?
```

```scala
println("Bruce has the powers: " + superPowersFor(bruce).mkString(", "))
println("Steve has the powers: " + superPowersFor(steve).mkString(", "))
println("Jane has the powers: " + superPowersFor(jane).mkString(", "))
  // NB mkString outputs a list in a user friendly format
}
```

Deconstruction Matches and Unapply
Scala Final Example

```scala
package s4j.scala.chapter18

class Customer(val name: String, val address: String)

object Customer {
  def unapply(customer: Customer): Option[(String, String)] = {
    Some((customer.name, customer.address))
  }
}
```

Map
Mapping Functions

```scala
package s4j.scala.chapter19

class Mappable[A](elements: List[A]) {

  def map[B](f: A => B): List[B] = {
    val result = collection.mutable.MutableList[B]()
    elements.foreach {
      result += f(_)
    }
    result.toList
  }
```

```scala
  // recursive version (with a nested def)
  def recur_map[B](f: A => B): List[B] = {
    def recur(head: A, tail: List[A]): List[B] = {
      tail match {
        case Nil => List(f(head))
        case _ => f(head) +: recur(tail.head, tail.tail)
      }
    }

    recur(elements.head, elements.tail)
  }

  // tail recursive version
  def tail_recur_map[B](f: A => B): List[B] = {
    def recur(accumulator: List[B], elements: List[A]): List[B] = {
      elements match {
        case Nil => accumulator
        case head :: tail => recur(accumulator :+ f(head), tail)
      }
    }

    recur(List[B](), elements)
  }
}

package map {
  object Example extends App {
    val numbers = List(1, 2, 54, 4, 12, 43, 54, 23, 34)
    val mappable = new Mappable(numbers)

    println(mappable.map(_ * 2))
    println(mappable.recur_map(_ * 2))
    println(mappable.tail_recur_map(_ * 2))
  }
}
```

FlatMap

```scala
package s4j.scala.chapter19

class FlatMappable[A](elements: A*) {

  def flatMap[B](f: A => List[B]): List[B] = {
    val result = collection.mutable.MutableList[B]()
    elements.foreach(element => {
      f(element).foreach(subElement => {
        result += subElement
      })
    })
    result.toList
  }

// abbreviated / alternative syntax (as shown in the book)
  def flatMapAbbr[B](f: A => List[B]): List[B] = {
    val result = collection.mutable.MutableList[B]()
    elements.foreach {
      f(_).foreach {
        result += _
      }
    }
    result.toList
  }
}

package flatmap {

  object Example extends App {
    def oddNumbersTo(end: Int): List[Int] = {
      val odds = collection.mutable.MutableList[Int]()
      for (i <- 0 to end) {
        if (i % 2 != 0) odds += i
      }
      odds.toList
    }
```

```
  val mappable = new FlatMappable(1, 2, 10)
  println(mappable.flatMap(oddNumbersTo))
  println(mappable.flatMapAbbr(oddNumbersTo))
 }
}
```

Syntax Cheat Sheet

Values

```scala
val x: Int = 42
var y: String = "mutable"
val z = "Scala FTW!"                         // using type inference
```

Functions

```scala
def add(x: Int, y: Int): Int = x + y        // single expression
def add(x: Int, y: Int) {                    // without =, Unit is
returned
  x + y
}
def min(x: Int, y: Int): Int = {            // last line = return value
  if (x < y)
    x
  else
    y
def min(x: Int, y: Int): Int = if (x < y) x else y
def min(x: Int, y: Int): Int = {            // but don't forget the
else
  if (x < y)
    x
  y                                          // bug!
```

```scala
def add(x: Int, y: Int) = x + y                  // return types can be
                                                 // inferred
def add(x: Int, y: Int = 2) = x + y              // default y to 2 if
                                                 // omitted
val add = (x: Int, y: Int) => x + y              // anonymous function
add(4, 2)                                        // call as usual

// convert an anonymous class (Ordering in this case) to a lambda
implicit def functionToOrdering[A](f: (A, A) => Int): Ordering[A] = {
  new Ordering[A] {
    def compare(a: A, b: A) = f.apply(a, b)
  }
}
```

Call-by-Name

```scala
def runInThread(task: => Int) {
  new Thread() {
    override def run(): Unit = task
  }.start()
}
```

Operator Overloading and Infix

```scala
5 * 10                                           // same as 5.*(10)
"Scala" replace("a", "*")
```

Classes

```scala
class Customer                                   // create a public class
class Customer(name: String)                     // with primary ctor
class Customer private(name: String)             // private constructor
private class Customer                            // a private class
private class Customer private(name: String)     // with private ctor
```

```scala
val c = new Customer("Bob")                    // create an instance
```

```scala
// class with primary constructor and auxiliary constructor
class Customer(forename: String, surname: String) {
  def this(surname: String) {
    this("Unknown", surname)
  }
}
```

Case Classes

```scala
case class Customer(name: String)              // a case class
case class Customer(val name: String)          // val is redundant here
```

```scala
// no need to use "new" to create a new instance with case classes
Customer("Bob")
```

```scala
// equality and hash code are free with case classes:
new Customer("Bob") == new Customer("Bob")     // returns true
```

Singleton Object

```scala
// a singleton instance
// when paired with a class, the object becomes a "companion" object
object Customer
```

Inheritance

```scala
class B extends A                              // subtype inheritance
class C(x: Int)
class D(value: Int) extends A(value)   // calling the super constructor
```

```scala
// overriding methods ("override" needed overriding non-abstract methods)
```

```
class E {
  def position: Int = 5
}
class F extends E {
  override position: Int = super.position + 1
}

// you can mixin in multiple traits but only one class (A)
trait SelfDescribing
trait Writable
class B extends A with SelfDescribing with Writable
class B extends SelfDescribing with A with Writable     // compiler failure
```

Fields

```
// name is not a field, it's available to the primary constructor only
class Customer(name: String)
// name is a public field (getter, no setter created)
class Customer(val name: String)
// name is a public field (getter and setter created)
class Customer(var name: String)
// name is a private field (a private getter is generated but no setter)
class Customer(private val name: String)
// name is private (a private getter and setter is generated)
class Customer(private var name: String)

customer.name_=("Bob")     // you can call the setter method directly
customer.name = "Bob"      // or use infix notation
```

Collections

```
val list = List(1, 4, 234, 12)              // create a list
val map = Map(1 -> "a", 2 -> "b")           // create a map
list.foreach(value => println(value))
list.foreach(println)
for (value <- list) println(value)
```

String Formatting

```
// String interpolation replaces '$' tokens with values
s"Customer name: $name USD"                    // Customer name: Bob
// Expression require additional parentheses
s"Customer basket value is $(customer.basket.value) USD"
// The 'f' prefix is like String.format
f"Square of 42 is ${math.sqrt(42)}%1.2f"       // Square of 42 is 6.48
"Escaping \"quotes\" is the same as in Java"
// triple quotes let you span rows and include quotes unescaped
""""vCard": {
      "id" : "007",
      "name" : "bond",
      "address" : "MI5"
   }"""
// The 'raw' string interpolator doesn't escape the usual escape chars
raw"a\nb"                                       // a\nb
```

Apply Method

```
val bob = Customer.apply("Bob")                // use as factory methods
val bob = Customer("Bob")                       // no need to call
explicitly

val array = Array(1, 54, 23, 545, 23)
array.apply(0)                                  // apply on array is a
"getter"
array(0)                                        // result is "1"
```

Update Method

```
val array = Array(1, 54, 23, 545, 23)
array(0)                                        // result is "1"
array.update(0, 34)
array(0)                                        // result is "34"
```

237

```
array(0) = 55                              // = is a shortcut to
update
array(0)                                   // result is "55"
```

Pattern Matching

```
value match {
  case 'R'              => ...   // literal match
  case Customer(name)   => ...   // constructor match (case classes)
  case x: Int           => ...   // type query match (ie instance of)
  case x: Int if x > 5 => ...   // with guard condition
  case (x, y)           => ...   // deconstruction using unapply
  case _                => ...   // default case
}

// same syntax is used with try/catch and exceptions
try {
  // ...
} catch {
  case e: MalformedURLException => println("Bad URL")
  case e: IOException => println(e.getMessage)
}
```

Covariance Types

Preserve the subtype relationship of Stack[Human] and Stack[Man] (where Man is a subtype of Human).

```
class Stack[+A] {
  ...
}
```

Example

```
class Human
class Man extends Human
class Woman extends Human

val people: Stack[Human] = Stack[Human]()
val men: Stack[Human] = Stack[Man]()              // ok
val women: Stack[Woman] = Stack[Human]()          // compiler error
```

Upper Type Bounds (extends)

```
A <: B says that type variable A extends B.
```

Contravariant Types

```
class Stack[-A] {
  ...
}
```

Lower Type Bounds (super)

B >: A says that B is a *super-type* of A. Usually A will be the type parameter of the class and B will be the type parameter of a method.

```
class Stack[+A] {
  def push[B >: A](b: B): Stack[B] = ...
}
```

Index

A

Abstract classes, 97, 99
Anonymous classes
    conversion to lambdas, 94
    creation, 82
    vs. functions, 68
Anonymous functions, *see* Lambdas/
        anonymous functions
AnyVal type, 22
AnyRef type, 24
Apply method, 143
Auxiliary constructors, 56–57

B

Bind, 184
Bottom types, 25
Bounded classes, 126
Bounded types, 127
Breaking control flow, 116

C

Call-by-name, 152–154, 234
Classes
    abstract, 97
    anonymous classes
        vs. anonymous functions, 68
        conversion to lambdas, 94
    bounded classes, 126

    stack class, 123
    without constructor
        arguments, 53
Class generics, 122
Closures *vs.* lambdas, 75, 157
Companion objects, 61
Conditionals
    ifs and ternaries, 105
    switch statements, 108
Constructors
    additional/auxiliary
        constructors, 56–57
    patterns, 162
    primary, 56–57
Contravariance of generic types, 34, 139
Covariant generic types, 34, 139
Curly braces and function literals, 149
Currying, 1, 154, 157

D

Deconstruction matches, 166
Default values, 35, 57
Diamond operator (<>), 122
Do and while loops, 113

E

Expression *vs.* statement, 106
Expressive Scala, 141
Extractor method, 168

T. Weston, *Scala for Java Developers*, https://doi.org/10.1007/978-1-4842-3108-1

Get the eBook for only $5!

Why limit yourself?

With most of our titles available in both PDF and ePUB format, you can access your content wherever and however you wish—on your PC, phone, tablet, or reader.

Since you've purchased this print book, we are happy to offer you the eBook for just $5.

To learn more, go to http://www.apress.com/companion or contact support@apress.com.

Apress®

Printed in the United States
By Bookmasters